Breaths That Count

*The True Story of a Boy, a Dolphin and
Their Remarkable Friendship*

Deena Hoagland

ISBN: 0615704948
ISBN-13: 9780615704944

Printed by CreateSpace

Forward

For nearly two decades I have been the Chief of Pediatric Cardiovascular Surgery at Miami Children's Hospital. As a father and a congenital heart surgeon, on most days I awake, kiss my children while they sleep and then go to work, where my cardiac team will help me open a dying baby's chest and try to rebuild a damaged or malformed heart. While we work, the child's mother waits outside, enduring an agony I can only imagine. The best moment of my day is seeing the relief in that mother's eyes when I tell her that her baby will be okay.

Deena Hoagland has been that mother.

In *Breaths That Count*, she describes her journey caring for a child with complex congenital heart disease. Hers is truly a unique story of tragedy, adventure, entrepreneurial innovation and healing.

I first met Deena when she entrusted my heart team with her son Joe's life. He has a complex congenital heart defect — *truncus arteriosus* — and has undergone multiple open heart operations, and interventional catheterizations, at several medical centers across the United States. Deena's journey to save her son's life has taken her from Denver to San Francisco to Miami, where she has seen the best and worst that American medicine can offer. Her intense determination to find the most effective care, partner with her son's medical teams, and create an innovative approach to his rehabilitation after a severe neurologic complication, are a testimony to her relentless devotion and creativity.

Deena's story will inspire and inform other families navigating complex medical treatments, as they engage in their own unique battles for their children's lives.

Breaths That Count takes the reader through the arc of Deena's son's treatment, from the first terrifying words — "It's his heart" — through the struggle to understand his anatomic problem, identify the right medical teams, and find a way to maneuver through the medical system. Deena clearly relates the desperation of living life five minutes at a time with a child close to death and the frustration of being told all the things her child will never do. She carefully interweaves the experiences of siblings, her husband, her relatives and friends as they endure Joe's struggle.

Deena then takes the reader into a completely unexpected aquatic realm when she sees her son make a powerful connection with a dolphin, and finds her epiphany — the ability to find joy no matter how out-of-control her life has become. Joe's therapeutic friendship with Fonzie becomes the sentinel event in Deena's and her husband's creation of Island Dolphin Care, a place where children with special needs can find joy and inspiration by swimming with dolphins. The story of Deena's relentless efforts to create, fund and sustain Island Dolphin Care, so that it could help thousands of other children from around the world, is a brilliant case study in entrepreneurial success.

Deena and Joe have a mystical connection to Fonzie, the dolphin who adopted him, and the other dolphins who, with their trainers, form an amphibious family. Deena relates the unique mammalian personalities, games and jokes they share, babies they name and raise, and the deaths they mourn. Deena lives in a world where humans and dolphins truly are one family. I have been to Island Dolphin Care and have seen my patients and their families laugh as they are pulled through the water, forgetting their troubles and being completely in the moment with these beautiful mammals. I will always be grateful to Deena for her remarkable achievement. She took the trauma and desperation of her fight for her son's life and turned it into a legacy for the future, a place where desperately ill children can touch a dolphin and experience pure joy.

As a congenital heart surgeon, my team often operates on "hopeless" children with lethal defects, and we wonder what good will come of our effort. Deena's son Joe was such a child. His ability to overcome repeated traumas and still find joy in life validates our efforts to save even the most hopelessly ill child. The Hoagland Family lesson is powerful: It is not our place to judge a child's potential; miracles do happen, so we never give up.

Redmond Paul Burke MD

This Is Where We Begin

Before we begin, my friend, Kate, told me I need to fill you in on a bit about myself and where I came from. So here goes: the first of us to arrive at Ellis Island from Poland was my Grandma Annie. An expert at sewing, she worked to bring the rest of her 11 siblings to America one by one. She also brought over her boyfriend from Lithuania. At the age of 16 they married and Grandpa Izzie built up one of the largest janitorial cleaning businesses in New York City.

My mother was born on the kitchen table. I didn't get the whole story, but I don't think they wanted to spill blood on the floor. I often wondered why they didn't just use the bathtub.

My mother, Miriam, married my father, Manny, who came from a Russian Orthodox Jewish family. They met in a bar in the Catskills; Mom was 35 and Dad was 46. They fell in love on their very first date and married three months later. Manny and his father went from selling roasted peanuts from pushcarts on the streets of New York City to owning a small grocery on the Lower East Side. He eventually supplied wholesale groceries to large businesses, hospitals and government agencies up and down the East Coast of the United States.

I was the younger of two children; my sister is four years older. We grew up in a sixth-floor walk-up apartment in

Queens. I never belonged there. I felt out of place, uncomfortable with the sounds of the buses and subway below. The rumble of the city never resonated with me. It was the country, animals and people that I loved.

There are two other things Kate said are important to tell you.

First, when I was at a family gathering, my cousins asked me what I wanted to be when I grew up. I didn't hesitate. I told them I was going to live on a farm, have lots of animals to care for and that I would also take care of all the children that nobody wanted.

I was five.

The second thing was when my parents were throwing a dinner party and one of their guests asked me the same question. I told them I loved the idea of wearing white go-go boots and dancing in a cage suspended from the ceiling of a Village nightclub called the DOM.

Later that evening my parents said to me, "Deena, what in the world are you thinking? You will marry a doctor or lawyer and live in a fine big house with many children . . . REALLY! Dancing in a cage!"

I was twelve.

Oh, also, Kate said not to forget the biggest part.

At the age of 22 I married Peter Hoagland. When I was 29 we had a daughter, Kate. And then, three years later, we had a son, Joe, who suffered a major stroke during one of his multitude of open-heart surgeries. An Atlantic bottlenose dolphin named Fonzie helped save his life.

He was three.

And this is where we begin . . .

PLUNGE

We are

I am

Submerged

We are the same

Endangered

This is/I am

Thought less

Stress less

Pain less

As long as I can

hold my breath

I can feel this way

I can see the pain

Free

Drifting

Weightless

Bubbles

You look

into my eyes

Connect our dreams

You move swiftly

Gracefully

Playfully

Dancing among

the waves

We tango briefly

For I am only human

Love recognizes no barriers.

It jumps hurdles, leaps fences, penetrates walls

to arrive at its destination

full of hope.

~ Maya Angelou

Part One: *Breaths That Count*

Synchronicity

As he surfaced to take a breath he noticed the boat and the men on it. Not thinking anything unusual he swam a bit closer to have a better look. What happened next changed each of our lives forever — so many lives altered by one breath.

One breath

Holding my belly and back, waddling through the parking lot, I knew this baby was asking to be born. For weeks now the contractions had been coming, strong and hard and then disappearing as if the last one was just my imagination. I kept hearing this child telling me it's time — time to be born. So I called the doctor and told him the contractions were ten minutes apart now and it was 9:00 pm. Should I stay where I was or come in to be checked? Certainly none of us needed another sleepless night. So we went in. After administering some medication and an IV he said he would check me again in the morning to see if there was any progress. In the morning the contractions were two minutes apart and I was not dilating. This was my second child. Just three years earlier the birth of my daughter required a C-section after 48 hours of hard labor. We weren't about to suffer through a repeat performance. I was sent down to the OR. This time I stayed awake and watched the birth, excited to meet this baby and hold him in my arms! The mirror in the room allowed me to watch in awe as they stretched my body apart and pulled him from me; tears of joy, amazement and gratitude rolling down my face. Pete's eyes met mine, smiling at the sound of his cry, the curly wet black hair and his long slick pink body. Amazing! They said they were just weighing him, doing the medical things they needed to do and would be right back. Of course Pete was with him; he had cut the cord and cleaned him — so proud. I drifted asleep content that my son would soon be in my arms. When I awoke I asked the nurse where my baby was. She assured me I had only just drifted asleep moments ago and they would be back with him soon. The next time I awoke I asked again and received the same answer, yet I thought surely some time must have passed. I took note of the time on the clock. When I awoke again to the same answer, this time I said, "No! It has not been moments. I want my baby! Where-is-my-husband-where-is-my-baby-get-them-now-you-are-lying-to-me!" And then they came. I was able to touch him with my index finger through the window in the isolette before they whisked him away.

Just one breath and our lives were changed forever. So many lives altered by one breath.

◊ ◊ ◊

No one knew for sure how old he was or why he was swimming alone. Because he was seemed so at ease, the veterinarians thought perhaps he had been in the company of humans before; but no one had any idea how this might have been. He took fish when offered, from the very beginning. Who was he? Where had he come from? And why was he alone? The men on the boat did not question it much more than those few fleeting thoughts; yet years later we are asking the very same questions. He was named for The Fonz, a character from *Happy Days,* a television sitcom about suburban teen life back in the 1950s. He seemed to have moxie — the type of personality that was sometimes scheming, bold and humorous.

◊ ◊ ◊

No one could give us much information about the diagnosis. The prognosis was not good either: Ninety percent of babies with *truncus arteriosus* die within the first year. Of the twelve babies that had undergone the heart surgery in Colorado, nine of them had not lived beyond the operation. No one knew where the other three were or if they were still alive. An attempt at surgical repair had been performed approximately 100 times. We located the surgeon who had done it the most — 45 times — in California. Our soap opera had begun, starring our little baby boy — "Fighter Joe" we called him, after his grandpa, a World War II bomber pilot. He looked tough. He *was* tough, but had a smile for everyone, always taking everything in stride. After all, he did not know life should be any different than it was. He was a calm baby who loved to be held and cuddled. The nurses enjoyed him and would keep him at the nurses' station even if I had to be gone for just a few minutes. Walking down the hall, I would see him propped up on a nurse's lap, pointing at everything and everyone. There was my brave boy smiling through the toughest of times. He was born with the personality necessary to get through this and teach all of us a lot about life.

◊ ◊ ◊

He chose his people — the ones he liked and those he did not. There are so many similarities, now that I think about it, between our lives. So much that we shared in common and yet lived species apart — worlds apart — he in the ocean and us on the land.

He was familiar with his environment and probably loved his life — free and carefree, capable of providing for himself. I, too, loved my life. I felt free to choose and decide on the things I wanted, where I lived and traveled, what I ate. I, too, took care of myself, independent and strong. Then just like surfacing for a breath, each of us took the next breath and our lives changed.

We were told that Fonzie adapted well, and quickly. From the very beginning he seemed to enjoy the people that swam or visited with him.

I adapted, too, but not so quickly; neither did the rest of my family. We all struggled trying to find our way through this tragedy, trying to get through each day without pain or sadness.

Joe and Fonzie both taught us about life and love and so much more.

Emancipation

The phone rings. It's Ronni, my best friend. She suggests that for our last hoorah before leaving for college we should work together as camp counselors. She still can't understand why I chose Denver. "God, it's so far away from here. I will never see you again!" she says with great drama. "Ronni, that's the whole idea!" I remind her that the only reason for going to Denver is because it's on the second page of the atlas. "No one can just pop in unannounced and visit me!" Every weekend while my sister Jane was in college, our parents would decide they had nothing better to do, so we would load up the car and drive four hours to Washington, D.C., to knock on her dorm door and "surprise" her. There was nothing more humiliating. I was not going to let that happen to me! I would give up the crown jewels for a life of my own. Ronni, however, was staying home to attend college in Queens. I couldn't bear the thought.

So off we go to a Jewish Camp in Upstate New York. I arrive to meet my campers: OMG! Eight little princesses who believe they are God's gift to the universe; after all, their parents tell them so at least five times each day. These girls drive me crazy and I think, "How will I ever get through this summer?" Ronni, on the other hand, has eight really cool

[13]

teens in her charge. They are listening to great music every time I go by her bunk, while I am having to yell, "Please stop picking on each other like that . . . Stop teasing her . . . Stop whining . . . Make your bed . . . Lights out!" I am going to go insane!

This is NOT my idea of a great summer before venturing off to college.

Standing in line just outside the mess hall, Ronni starts squealing with excitement. Jumping up and down she points out the guy she thinks she is in love with. "Oh, please! You've got to be kidding me!" I tell her. "For God's sake, Ron, he's wearing platform shoes like the guy in *Dirty Dancing*. Who does he think he is?" I tell her emphatically, "If you go out with him I will not be able to stand it for even one minute. He is a total loser!" One week later they're in love! "Please, God, help her!"

No answer from God.

One week goes by and I cannot take another second of the whining eight-year-olds while watching Ronni destroy the rest of her life. I quit! On the drive back to the city I blast the music in my car and plan my next move. The next morning I go right over to the new deli on Queens Boulevard where there's a "WAITRESS WANTED" sign in the window. I ask for as many shifts as they can give me. They're happy to oblige.

"Pastrami sandwich on pumpernickel, don't forget the mustard," every customer barks. I serve so much pastrami that I know I'll never eat it again. But I manage to save enough money for my trip west. I call two friends and ask if they want to get out of town, then I pack my car and suitcases for college. With my parents in Europe, I leave a note on the kitchen counter: "Sorry, have to go. Don't worry. I will call you from Denver!" There it is. I was never more excited than for this adventure!

For the next two months we camp across the U.S. with the plan that, in September, I will drive myself to the dorm and check in. I call my parents every other day to make sure they know I'm okay, but I can tell it's hard for them. I arrive at my co-ed dorm in time for orientation but don't go. I'm thrilled when the weekends come and my parents are not knocking on my door!

I go home for the first Thanksgiving holiday and Ronni is waiting. She's ecstatic. "Wait till you hear my news!" she says, jumping up and down. Oh No, I'm thinking. Where have I heard this before? "Calm down. Whoa, Nellie. What's going on?" I can't believe my ears: she and Morris (that's the guy's name, the guy with the platform shoes) are getting married.

"What? Are you crazy? I told you not to go out with him!" OMG! I can't wait to get back to Denver. That will be the last time I go home before introducing my future husband, Peter, to my family in nothing less than a scene right out of a Woody Allen film.

Dogs, love and driveways

I fell in love with Colorado, amazed by how beautiful the campus was and how crazy the people in my dorm were. They all acted as though they had never been away from home before. The mountains astounded me. For days I would look at them convinced they were clouds. Then it finally sunk in: no more New York! At last I grasped — finally understood — that song about America: *O beautiful for spacious skies*. I felt at home. My classes were ridiculously easy. I made so many friends but, as usual, I felt very different from the others. I knew from my camp days with my bunkmates that I fit in, but there has always been a degree of separation. My friends would often tell me to quit thinking so much, or they made comments about what the heck I might conjure up next.

But there was always something new to do. I was excited about everything! In their preppy state of mind, it seemed like a lot of the people in the dorm were quite content to just hang out, while I was busting at the seams to experience everything my new world offered, including the handsome young *goyishe* men I had never dated before. I soon grew bored with dorm life and got myself a dog. Kamala was her name. She was a cross between a golden retriever and who knows what. After renting a few off-campus houses with friends, I decided to take on the mountains and moved into a beautiful cabin with an eye-level view of Mount Evans. The highest mountain, it remained capped in snow all year-round.

It was ten in the morning and one of my roommates, Patty, would be coming out of class any minute. She told me to be standing on the steps of the general classroom building. She would walk outside with him and introduce us.

[16]

She had told me the night before that she had met my future husband! I was not looking for a husband then — the furthest thing from my mind — but there I was, curious, standing on the steps waiting as I had been told. They had grown up just yards from each other, yet had never met until recently. How strange that they found each other in a classroom of 300 students! I had no idea that our meeting was going to be one of those life-changing moments. I don't know if he would remember that meeting the way I do. I can still recall the way his hair was tied back in ponytail, and thinking that his eyes were smiling. I felt my insides stir and wondered if he felt the same, but he didn't give me any clues that he did. Who knew then what would come to us; the way our lives would entangle and unravel? Who knew? I have had breathless moments in my life — I suppose everyone does — moments when, as they are happening, the stirring inside my body knows way before my head does that THIS IS BIG — BIGGER than I could have ever imagined.

I was 17 then, still a teenager. The thought of spending time together made me smile, feel excited, not knowing what might happen next. I could feel my face go flush. He was different from any guy I had ever dated. Everything was different. We stood and talked a few minutes. I had no idea how old he was or what he was studying. I didn't even know his last name.

I can't remember what was said other than we talked about our dogs. I had time between classes so I offered to take his dog for a run in the park. After that I didn't see him much but would always go by his house when bringing

"Mala," my dog, to the park and as I had suggested I would walk and play with Sam, his springer spaniel. He always left his door open and was never home when I was there so I would leave notes on his desk. He never called me and I didn't see him for many months. Then one Friday afternoon I ran into my friend Debbie on campus. She invited me to a party at her house that night. I didn't intend to go, but she saw that I was already thinking about my drive up to the cabin and a weekend alone. She told me she knew I was dodging her and asked me to come for just a little bit. At the end of the day I decided to stop by after all. I really liked them and it promised to be a good party. It was.

There he was at the opposite end of the room, leaning against the wall, drink in hand. When I came through the doorway he saw me and grinned. That was when I first noticed the stirring in him. We talked all night; first about our dogs and then about everything under the sun. It was late and I had a long drive ahead of me, but before I left I told him where I lived and how to find the cabin. I hoped he would come and see me sometime. As I drove up the canyon I thought about how kind and gentle he seemed to be, his eyes quiet and happy. He was interesting. Talking to him was easy and we had talked for hours.

In the morning I awoke to the smell of the evergreen trees. The western tanagers, perhaps the most beautiful bird in the world, were hopping from one tree to the next outside my window. I could still see traces of snow on Mount Evans from my living room window. I heard a car coming up the long road and wondered who was visiting the neighbor so early in the day. They never had visitors this early on the weekend. As the car approached I went about my usual routine and when the engine stopped I never turned to see who was there until I heard a knock on the screen door. Bewildered, I turned and saw him standing there. I felt my heart jump and wondered if he knew what I was feeling. Was I being obvious? Thinking about it makes me smile. It was so much fun and I felt that finally I was living my life just for me.

We had a great day. We hiked, ate a picnic lunch and then he left because he said he had things to do in town. We started hanging out a lot. I was infatuated. He was such a nice guy and so quiet. But whenever he spoke he talked about such "heavy" stuff. Our backgrounds were so different — he had gone to an expensive boarding school. He told me his friends called him "Heavy Pete," not simply because he was a big guy, but because he was a big thinker. I finally learned his last name was Hoagland — Peter Hoagland. Soon after that he told me he was dating a girl who lived in Idaho. I told him I was seeing a guy who went to school in Oregon. We called each other often and attended parties together knowing that we each had someone else in our life, someone special but far away. My feelings were in opposition. I tried to deny my attraction to him because I didn't think he was feeling the same way about me — he had a girlfriend, after all. But there were times I found myself secretly hoping he was just as attracted to me. If he was just a friend, why was I thinking about him so much? But even stranger, why was I thinking about him when I already had a boyfriend? Was it just because I was lonely? Or did I *really* like him? I didn't know the answer. All I knew was that we had become such great friends during my freshman year.

One night my roommates and I decided to throw a party. Peter came and had a few drinks — actually more than a few. There was a roaring fire in the fireplace and he was leaning against the wall. I was aware he was watching me and I was certainly watching him. At the end of the night everyone else had gone home and he was still leaning against the wall. Suggesting he was too drunk to drive, I asked if he wanted to stay. He agreed, but never made a move. (Darn it!) I wasn't going to assume that he wanted to sleep with me, so I brought a pillow and blanket and placed them on the couch. The next morning he left quickly. It was awkward. It seemed like he couldn't get away fast enough and I was confused. I didn't see or hear from him for days.

There was a party in the mountains I had heard about so I went. When I arrived, there he was with another girl! Oh no, that must be his girlfriend, I thought. When he was alone for a moment I went up to him and said, "Hey, where have you been? I've missed you." He gave me a blank look, unlike any other time we had talked and told me he had been busy "doing stuff." When I said why not come by sometime and hang out, he answered abruptly, "And sleep on the couch? No thanks!" I was stunned and walked away angry. Really! What a jerk!

But the next day, I felt badly about the way things had gone. Pete had once told me he loved rhubarb and strawberry pie, so I made one and took it to his house. I left it on his desk with a note apologizing for whatever it was that had made him angry. I told him I was confused by what he had said and that I was unsure of what he wanted from me — just a friendship or something more?

Early the next morning I heard a car coming up the road; the car door slammed and there was a knock on my door. He was standing in the doorway with the empty pie plate. He smiled. I took one look at him and knew exactly what I was feeling. He made the first move — that was the one thing that I was never going to do!

We were together throughout my sophomore year. Then one day he told me that he and a good friend were ditching school to take off for Mexico to surf and he didn't know how long he'd be gone. I was distraught at the thought of his leaving because I had allowed myself to fall in love and I thought that he loved me too. This Mexico trip confused me. I had been telling myself that I didn't want to be in a serious relationship anyway, and that it should be okay for him to leave — you know, all the things you're supposed to think and believe about keeping it casual. I did everything I could to convince myself that his Mexico trip was a good thing, but my heart was sad as I waved goodbye. When he drove away with his surfboard on top of the Volkswagen van, I was telling myself how cool it had been just to love him *this* long.

A few weeks later, Pete called from Mexico. "Hey, spring break's coming up. Want to fly to Mazatlan and I'll pick you up? We can spend a few weeks together." I was on the phone purchasing a ticket within minutes! I thought I was crazy. What in the world was I thinking? But I did it anyway.

After three weeks in Mexico I was home again, alone. Ugh! I tried to go out with other guys, but I couldn't help making comparisons and wishing Pete was back in Denver. Weeks later, it was my birthday and his car pulled into the driveway. He had decided to come home! I was ecstatic. But when we woke up the next morning and he told me he was leaving for Idaho, my heart fell. I was thinking: Holy Crap! I must need to learn some lessons about saying good-bye? I was getting better at it, for sure. Peter, as planned, left again and I went on as before. Besides, I was now in my senior year of college and needed to concentrate on school. Over the next couple of months we exchanged a few letters and some phone calls, but I missed him. I thought this time we were *really* over. It seemed as though he planned on staying in Idaho for good. Then, when I least expected it, he called and asked, "Want to come for a visit? I miss you."

Before I knew it, my faithful dog Kamala and I were on a plane. It was so great to be in his arms again. It felt electric and right, but I knew in my heart that he was happy there, especially when he told me he had put a deposit on a house — a gentleman's farm on Jewel Lake. We drove to see it and it was spectacular; so beautiful and just what he had always wanted. His friend Rick lived there too, so he already had someone to hang out with. Rick was building a house for himself and Pete was helping him.

That night Rick let us sleep in the bunkhouse. Early the next morning I woke up to the sound of roosters crowing. I sat and looked out the window, knowing in my heart that at the end of this trip we would probably say our last good-bye. He looked into my eyes and said, "I can't stay here alone." I assured him that his place was beautiful and that he would be all right. What was he talking about? He was a confident guy. He certainly didn't need my reassurance. But I was lost in my own dialogue about why I was there and I wasn't listening to what he was really trying to say. "What do you mean?" I asked.

Before I could make sense of it all, he said, "I mean, I need you. Will you stay here with me . . . marry me?"

I couldn't believe my ears. This is *not* what I was expecting — not then, and not from *him*! I told him that I loved him, but I didn't think I could live in Sandpoint, Idaho. "You have to remember, I'm a city girl. I love the countryside, but this is *wilderness*."

We spent the day in town getting supplies. I looked at the people in the Payfair Market and was scared to death. That night I told him that I loved him so much, but if he were just to take one look at the women shopping in Payfair he would know that I would never fit into this town.

I told him, "They have five children hanging from their carts, Wonder Bread and frozen dinners, Twinkies and Rice-A-Roni, and I would probably be the only Jew in town!" I knew that no matter how strong our love was, I didn't think it could survive in this small town in the middle of Nowhere, USA. This goodbye was by far the saddest because I was finally convinced we were not really meant to be together.

When I returned to Denver I told myself that now I would have to move on. I wasn't about to buy another plane ticket just to follow him wherever his next whim took him.

[23]

Weeks later I was on the phone with my friend Kate. I was expecting my cousins to arrive to take me to dinner, so when I heard a car in the driveway I told her I had to go. But it was Pete who was standing at the screen door. *Deja vu*. Stunned, I couldn't move. It was Pete who opened the door. "There was no reason for me to stay if you're not going to be there with me." He had come back to Colorado to be with me.

Smoking drinks, scorpions and courage

It was 2:00 am when I finally summoned the courage to call them. I had been at Trader Vic's drinking their signature drink, the "smoking scorpion," and celebrating my twenty-first birthday, but I wasn't too drunk — just drunk enough to help me place the call. I had never planned to marry him; when we started going out, I just wanted to be with him and have a good time. The thought of marrying never came into things — at least not until we realized we were truly in love and meant to be together for the rest of our lives.

She answered. It was the sobering moment.

"Mom?"

"Is everything all right? What's the matter? It's two in the morning! Why are you calling me?"

Deep breath, "Mom, remember Peter?"

"Yes," she said. "Why are you calling me at two in the morning?"

"Mom, we are going to get married. Peter asked me to marry him."

"Oh . . . ? Well, that's nice. What's his last name dear?"

[24]

I can still hear her voice, bewildered and confused. The sheets rustled as she sat up in bed.

"His name is Peter Hoagland, Mom. You met him the last time you visited. Remember?"

"Yes," she said. "I remember. Is he from Rumson, New Jersey?"

"Yeah, he is, Mom. How do you know that?"

"Well, we'll talk in the morning."

Silence. Click.

Everything happens for a reason. Everything was aligning perfectly. I did not understand that yet.

Peter's grandfather owned a lot of real estate in New York City. My grandfather owned an office-cleaning and janitorial business in New York City. My grandfather was his grandfather's janitor. At least that is how they saw it: another sort of Romeo and Juliet.

Let's just say there was tension.

His family wrote him letters, suggested he was being neurotic. How could he marry a Jewish princess from New York? What was he thinking? Didn't he realize we had nothing in common?

My family began writing my obituary.

As my parents' little "Miss Jewish American Princess," I realized I was trading the crown jewels for this man. I was happy and relieved not to ever carry that burden again. Giving up the princess crown was such a relief. I had already broken all the rules — this one being the last. There was nothing else I could possibly do to make them unhappy. I had never followed their rules or met their expectations, not ever. Somehow they always found a way to love and accept me just the way I was, anyway; all the while knowing I was different. I know now that I broke their mold.

I came home to talk to both of them, but especially my father. My mother thought this might be the best thing to do. She said, "He is so upset, he doesn't know what to do! Maybe you should come home and try to talk to him yourself. I am trying but he is not listening to me."

So I flew home to try.

When I arrived he was in the bedroom, "lying down," she said. "That is all he wants to do these days, is lie down and go to sleep. But I know he is not sleeping," she said with a cluck of her tongue. Mom and her mother, Grandma Annie, always made that sound when they were anxious and unsure of themselves, or exhale with a sigh under the breath, "*Oy vey ismir*, God should help me now!"

"I'll go get him and tell him you're here," as if he didn't already know that. They live in a tiny apartment on the sixth floor; of course he heard the elevator and the front door open. He knew I was there but chose to be dramatic and stay in his room, as if that was going to make me change my mind!

Okay, God, now would be your chance to help me, I thought.

He emerged from the bedroom wearing his bathrobe, unshaven, *yamaka* on his head. He said "Hello" with his eyes cast down. He could hardly look at me and I could see he was struggling with his emotions. He was too proud a man to show his emotions openly. I don't know that he ever did, even with my mother in private. But today he wore them on his sleeve as a Jewish mourner wears the torn black ribbon. I was struggling too. I never intended to hurt him. I was just living my life. He motioned to the dining table to sit down. My mother gave me a peck on the cheek and retreated to the kitchen saying, "I will give you two some privacy," but I knew full well that she had her ear to the swinging door, hoping neither of us saw that it was open just a crack.

"So *nu*?" he said. "What should we do now?"

"Dad," I said, "you always told me to stand up for what I believe in my heart, right? So I have to do it now too. I didn't do this to hurt you. It just happened. When I met Pete we were friends. I never thought we would fall in love, but we did, and now I have to listen to my heart."

He did not look at me, his head held down, and I could tell his heart was heavy. I knew he loved me more than anything. I could see his pain and it was so heart wrenching. We came from different cultures, in different times with different values. We were both living in different worlds; he still in the old world.

"Dad, what is a good Jewish man?" I asked. "Tell me the qualities that a good Jewish man has."

He began the list for me, reciting what I had heard so many times before at this very table.

"So," he would say, "you will marry a good Jewish man — a doctor, a lawyer perhaps — from a good Jewish family. You won't have to worry about anything. You will have money, children. Good Jewish men do not drink too much. They do not cheat on their wives. They do not hit their wives

[27]

or children. They are gentlemen. They do not get divorced. One day when you grow up," he would say, "you will marry a good Jewish boy, from a good Jewish family and I will dance at your wedding!"

And now, he exclaimed, "So, you couldn't find a nice Jewish man in all of Denver?"

I listened, and then I told him, "Peter is honest. He's a hard worker. He loves me. He will not cheat on me. He does not drink too much. He knows how to fix everything and can build anything. He has so many talents. He's really smart, too. Dad, I know if you would meet him that you would really like him." Then I asked, "How can you hold it against him if he was delivered to the wrong house?"

Finally, he looked me right in the eye. "What?"

I said, "Pete has all of the qualities that you always told me to look for in a man. What if he has a Jewish heart and was just delivered to the wrong house? Can you blame him for that? Will you blame him for being born to Episcopalians? Won't you try, Dad? If you met him I know you would like him. I know if you gave him a chance you would see he has a Jewish heart and mind."

He was holding his head in both his hands now. I could tell he was really trying. I had tested his beliefs and every cell in his body. He looked at me. Then he asked, "So, will you get married by the rabbi?"

I answered without hesitation, "No, Dad, we can't. It would not be fair to his family."

Angrily he rallied back as if in a heated tennis match, "You're getting married by a priest! I am writing your obituary! What did I ever do to deserve this?" he cried, looking skyward, as if pleading with God.

I waited a moment, then met his eyes and answered him in a soft voice, hoping he would strain to listen to each syllable as I made my final point, hoping he would finally acquiesce.

"Dad, we can't get married by a priest or a rabbi. We can't offend his family or ours."

"Then how will you get married?"

With that, my mother practically fell into the dining room! "Oh!" she exclaimed. "The neighbor downstairs — you know, Manny, the family in 5-F — well, their daughter just married a *goy*, too. She said they married at the country club. They were married by a judge, a Jewish judge!" I could tell she had it already figured out and was just waiting for the right moment to interject, all the while allowing him to keep his pride and power.

"A Jewish judge?" he said, and both my mother and I knew at that very moment we had won that round.

"So why don't we have some bagels and coffee?" she said. "We can talk about meeting your Peter and his family. What do you think, Mendel?"

"Okay" he said. "I am thinking about it."

Mom turned to me, whispering, "It will be all right, you will see. You did right. What you said was right. It will be okay, it will be okay. Let me be the one to tell your grandmother. It will be okay now."

Pete's family wasn't exactly thrilled with the prospect of having me in their family either. His brother said to him, "You know if our dad were still alive this would never be happening!" His mother sent family members to Denver to check me out. She asked if she could invite her minister to marry us in the bridal suite before the wedding. Pete said, "No, Mom, we can't. Deena promised her father she would not do that."

When introduced to Peter's aunt, Mary, she said, in her matter-of-fact way, "I think you are just what Peter needs! You're smart and I think it is possible that you are the best thing that ever happened to him!"

Then, under her breath she added, "If Hase likes you, you will have it made, and I am sure she will find you enchanting!" Hase was the nurse hired to care for Peter's mother just after her birth in Japan. They were living in Japan because her father was the ambassador. Hase remained with the family, raised Peter's mother, and for all practical purposes was the only "grandmother" that Peter and his siblings ever knew. It turned out that Aunt Mary was right. Hase did come to love me and I her.

In the end, both families decided we were going to marry with or without their approval, so they chose to make the best of what appeared to each side to be a temporary situation.

How amazing my parents were, to find a way within their religious boundaries to let me be who I was. I still wonder when it was that they came to realize this and to let me go. It's obvious to me now that they did just that.

[30]

The morning of the wedding I was nauseous. My knees buckled every time someone asked if I was nervous. I did not think I would ever get through the day. When it was time to get ready for the ceremony, my sister and mother were so busy primping each other that no one was around to help me. We had decided on a small wedding and neither of us had attendants. I finally called out to Pete and he came and helped me into my gown. We were standing together, both families waiting for the music to begin. We walked down the aisle together and stood in front of the judge. Our mothers' eyes met and they both whispered under their breath, "The grandparents are turning in their graves. If they were alive surely this would never be happening!"

Pete and I wrote our own ceremony. When the judge began to speak, the piano player got up to get himself a drink, thinking it was going to be awhile. By the time he got back we had already said "I Do" and were kissing. There was an awkward moment, as no one knew exactly what to do. Then, surprising all of us, every one of the guests stood and gave us a standing ovation!

Kittredge — Listening to the trees

Standing on the mountain overlooking the small town, I thought life was perfect. I could listen to the sound of the wind in the trees forever. We built our house on dreams and love. Its foundation contained a time capsule stuffed with half-torn tickets from our favorite concerts and photos of us, young and in love.

While Pete was hammering the stairs, I crawled underneath and etched within a heart, "Deena loves Pete, Pete loves Deena". I envisioned our children playing there with dolls or toy cars and seeing it, always a part of their lives.

I cannot remember ever feeling afraid when I was there with Pete. We had everything we wanted: great friends, a beautiful place to live, enough money and no worries. I became pregnant with our first child and we were both so excited. It was the right time and also a great time for both of us. Pete and I danced to Bob Marley while he hammered away or while I was cooking. We spent each weekend building our dream house, one that he designed and was hand-building himself. Each evening he would ask, "What room should we sleep in tonight?" He would bring out the sleeping bags or a makeshift bed and set up our "bedroom" for the night, a can of wildflowers beside us as we watched the shooting stars.

When the roof was finally put on and the interior walls went up, we moved in. We knew we would be working on that house for years to come, but that didn't matter to either of us because we loved being there. It was our house and every nook and cranny carried a special finishing touch that was part of us.

Indian summer came, my favorite time of the year when the days are long, the wildflowers in full bloom and the skies so vast. My belly was so large I could no longer see my toes when standing up! After work one day I felt the contractions begin. I could not wait to get home to tell Pete it was time to meet our baby. If I had only known that 48 hours later I would still be huffing and puffing I am sure I would not have been as enthusiastic as I was early that evening. One C-section later, Kathryn Elisabeth arrived, beautiful and healthy, weighing in at seven-and-a-half pounds and twenty-one inches long. Up until the moment I met her we had decided that if the baby were a girl we would name her Hannah and call her "Annie" after my grandmother; but the moment I first held her I called her "Kate." Pete looked at me with surprise, "What happened to 'Hannah'?"

In a matter-of-fact way, I replied, "Well, look at her, Honey. She doesn't look one bit like a 'Hannah.' She looks like a 'Kate'!"

Our house was filled with love and joy. For the next three years we celebrated every day. Kate was the most adorable baby. People stopped us wherever we went and would comment on how beautiful she was. Once, while shopping in a Coach store, I was looking at a shoulder bag that I really liked. I put it down and told the saleslady that I would have to think about it, as it was a little more than I wanted to spend. Suddenly, a little voice called out from the stroller, "Charge it!" It was hard to believe she could be so precocious!

Pete was selling real estate then and building passive-solar houses and room additions. He was often able to work at home and be with Kate. I had finished my master's degree in clinical social work and was working as a therapist in private practice. Our house was the social center for all of our friends; there was always room for anyone. When it snowed we would invite everybody for a ski party out our back door. There would be a big pot of soup on the stove and a roaring fire. We would take turns skiing down the hill and driving the truck to haul people back up. It was our winter wonderland. I should have known better than to think life could stay that way.

I kept a journal of when the crocus would push through the dirt to greet spring. I knew when the last snow fell each year, when the aspens would turn, when the evening grosbeak would return and the hummingbirds reappear. From my shower window I watched the western tanagers hop from tree to tree. My friends would ask whether we would have an early or late spring. They knew I kept track and would have a good idea. I should have known, just by watching the world as closely as I did, that nothing stays the same. Storms would come, trees would fall; there was new growth and I watched as old growth died. That's nature. That's life.

Why should I expect my life to be different? Was it because my mother and father always told me I had nothing to fear or worry about in my life? Having survived the Depression to become successful and financially secure, they often reminded me that they had lived through the worst, so that in my life I would have nothing to worry about.

If only I had listened closer to the trees I might have been more prepared for what was to come.

In graduate school I learned that one in every ten children is born with a disability. When my friends and I began to have babies we wondered if that statistic would prove true in our little group, never once thinking it would apply to me. Then I forgot.

Capezios, pumps and pearls

I loved driving into the city to work, and I loved driving home to the mountains at the end of my day. I loved my navy leather briefcase — somehow that represented success to me. I *was* a success. I had a beautiful little girl, a wonderful husband, a big house on the mountain, a nanny, an office and people were asking me to give lectures about my counseling practice and treatment methods. It was an exciting and fun time. Pete enjoyed his work. He loved fishing and skiing. He was the president of the Evergreen Chapter of Trout Unlimited, a 37-year-old volunteer organization devoted to maintaining and improving the fisheries and environment in the U.S. I enjoyed meeting people and entertaining. We joined the health club. I worked out in the mornings while Kate went to the nursery. Then she would go to preschool and I would go to work in the city. I loved my briefcase, my matching Capezios, flannel suits and pearls. This is the way it is supposed to be.

I spoke to my mother every day on the phone. It seemed that the birth of Kate gave her a new purpose in life. I think her purpose for living was to be a grandmother. I had never seen her happier. Everywhere she went she would pull out a photo album and show every picture of her brilliant and beautiful grandbaby.

Then the phone call came from my mom — she was sick and going in for tests. It didn't look good. There were spots on her lungs. The results showed a very aggressive oat cell cancer. The test results came on my thirtieth birthday and we went to be with my parents in New York. The prognosis was a shock: "Eight weeks," the doctor said. We begged them to come home with us and spend whatever time she had left with all of us together. But they both said "No. When God gives you this, your obligation is to do whatever you can to be well; to live and never give up hope for life."

My father said, "God is testing us."

So they decided to try chemotherapy. I traveled to New York every few weeks with Kate for special visits. I was there when my mother's hair fell out and when she fell into a puddle of sobs over the sink. We went to the wig shop but, truthfully, even without her hair she was beautiful.

For 18 months I watched her be a warrior, fighting so hard to live. She wanted to be Kate's grandma. "I am going to dance at her wedding," she would say. But I watched her begin to lose: First her hair; then her weight — down to 90 pounds — then her strength, her ability to eat, to talk. She looked at the world through sunken eyes. Then twenty-one days before she died, she phoned: "Deena I am having a party and I want you to come."

"A party! I don't understand, Mom. How can you have a party now? You are sick. I don't feel like a party, Mom. You are so sick. You are dying, Mom!" I was sad. I was angry and in disbelief. What was she thinking?

[36]

"Deena, I am not dead yet. Don't bury me yet. How dare you!" she said angrily. "Listen here, young lady, the music is still playing for me. I am going to dance. I am going to see my friends. I am going to buy a beautiful new dress. I *am* having a party and I want you to come!"

I could not believe my ears. But this time I could not disappoint her. I would play by her rules. I bought Laura Ashley mother-daughter dresses for Kate and I and new Capezios to match. We arrived to see her looking beautiful in a blue silk dress. Her blue eyes shone bright that night. She went to her party in a wheelchair but left it at the door. She danced with my father and as they glided over the floor he carried her, whispered to her, and I could see they both needed this last dance together. At the end of the evening we tucked her into bed. The next day she could not get out of bed. Pete would carry her to the bathroom and to the table to sit but she would not eat. She told Pete she adored him. "I'm sorry I ever doubted you." She did not get out of bed the next day or any day after that.

"She's dying, Dad. You need help now."

"What kind of help?" he asked. "She is not dying. She is just tired. You will see. She will be fine."

"No, Dad, she is dying. You need to get help, for both of you. Please, Dad, can't you see? She is not going to give up because she does not want to disappoint you. She needs help now, to die. And you need help, to let her go. Please, Dad, let me help you."

"You cannot come here and tell me what to do! You cannot say that word in my house! You will *not* say that word! She is not going to die!" He sobbed and sobbed, sitting at the kitchen table, holding his head in his hands.

I called hospice. They brought nurses, someone to bathe her, medicate her, and keep her comfortable. That is what she wanted now. I bought her Elizabeth Arden lotion, her favorite scent, and massaged her failing body. She was resting now, so we went home. The next day my father fired hospice. He told the nurse he found a treatment for her, to save her. He took her to another doctor for experimental treatment — a new chemo that went directly to her brain. Dad said, "It is the miracle I have prayed for. You will see. She will be better soon." A few days later he phoned, crying. He said that during the night she had to go to the bathroom. Dad tried to take her and she fell. "I couldn't lift her off the floor." They spent the rest of the night on the floor in the hallway. He told me that once morning came he phoned the doctor and an ambulance took her to the hospital. She was paralyzed. She could not talk anymore either. He held the phone to her ear as I said, "Mom, I love you. I am sorry I am not there. I don't want you to suffer anymore, Mom. It's okay to die."

The music stopped. She died April 21. She would not want me sitting *shiva* on my birthday. It was her last gift to me I thought.

I was pregnant again and we were filled with mixed emotions as we watched my belly swelling with life while making arrangements for my mother's funeral.

Dad said, "Pregnant women are not allowed at funerals. It is bad luck. "It's against Jewish law!" We were there anyway. After all, hadn't I already broken most of those J-laws anyway? With Kate in my arms I sat in the chapel. I could not let her go. I looked at the pine box. I told her everything I wanted her to know. I understood she needed to go. I whispered to her, "Mom, watch over me, watch Kate grow."

Once home I called my dad every day. With Mom gone I began to realize how much he had depended on her. He was angry she died. She was 12 years younger than he and he never expected life or God would do this to him. He always thought that he was going to die first. He sat in the living room staring at the walls, waiting for the phone to ring. He did not know anyone's phone number. They were all "in her head."

He would say, "Your mother would have done that for me . . . She would know where that is . . . She would know what to do now."

The locker room, karma and dreams for the future

My friend Dyan and I stood by the lockers drying off after our usual workout, comparing our swollen bellies, cravings and the new baby names we were contemplating. Except today she looked different. "What's wrong? I asked. She began to cry long sad slow tears, the ones that are full of sorrow.

"What's wrong?" What could possibly be wrong?

She led me to a bench where we sat as her story unfolded: Her placenta may be insufficient; her baby may not be getting the proper nutrition to grow. She said the doctor told them to prepare for the baby to be small and underdeveloped, possibly brain damaged. I listened.

"What do I do?" she asked. "How do I go on?"

All of the questions kept pouring from her heart — and from mine. I stood, still drying off. Where were my clothes? Picking up my socks and pulling them on, I heard myself saying, "You just go on. You find a way. You eat, sleep and do everything that is in your control to help your baby now. And when she or he is born, there will be more questions and answers but you will find the power to answer them. Whatever this baby needs you will get. You will find ways to nurture this baby one day at a time. Right now none of the answers are in your control so you have to keep moving forward as if everything is okay. The answers that you need will be there for you when you need them."

I can hear myself saying those words to her now, as if it were just this morning that we were standing there drying off as we did almost every morning at the club. We had been through a lot together. Our daughters were the same age in the same preschool class. We both had miscarriages at the same time last year and now here we are again with babies so close to being born. I was sad . . . and guilty in a way, because everything about this pregnancy was so perfect for me. I told her to be brave. I guess I had to tell her that. What else could I do? What other choice did I have?

We were just six weeks away from having our babies — hers was due first. "We are close to the end," I said. "We will know soon and then you will know what this baby needs and you will provide it."

And so her beautiful daughter Ariel was born small and healthy. We rejoiced!

How she had worried. She thanked me for my support. It's hard to know how to be supportive in those very uncomfortable times and situations. It's like when someone dies, what do you say? Is there anything that you can say that could possibly make it better? I don't really think there is a right thing to say — nothing can take the pain away. Maybe the best thing to do is just to listen and say simply, "I am so sorry."

When Joe was born, weeks later, I was in an unbelievable twist. How can this be? My world had just collapsed. It never occurred to me to think back to that morning in front of the lockers, but it did to Dyan. After Joe was born she visited, brought flowers and food. She was there for me when it seemed that others were not.

It was a year later that she shared with me that even though she knew it was impossible and that her thoughts were crazy, she still had them: that somehow that morning God knew that she could not cope with being the mother of a disabled child, and so the disabled child needed another kind of nurturing, and they switched! She said God heard us talking in front of the lockers, heard my wisdom and saw her fear and uncontrollable anxiety.

So the babies' souls were switched. She felt guilty. I could see that her feelings were real to her. I didn't know how to answer her. I didn't believe it possible, but somehow I had to acknowledge her feelings. I was numb. I did know that the same words that I shared with her that morning helped me get through so many minutes and hours of uncertainty, and I guess they still do. Maybe I needed to hear those words myself. It was my own advice that I had to live by now — my own lessons that had to get me through.

◊ ◊ ◊

I never understood courage until Joe came. I had never really truly understood sadness. As a therapist, that's a weird thing for me to say. But the day Joe was born my world turned upside down.

The contractions had begun much too early in my pregnancy. I called the doctor and when he saw me he prescribed medication that would stop the labor, because what I was experiencing was the real thing. I took one pill and thought I could feel my heart pounding outside my body! The doctor told me to stay in bed. So for a few weeks that is what I did. Three weeks before my actual due date, the contractions grew steady and hard. We went in for a checkup and the doctor kept me in the hospital overnight. He said he wanted to monitor the contractions through the night and in the morning he would decide what to do. The next morning he wanted to do a C-section because I was not progressing, just as with Kate's labor. "So," he said, "let's have this baby *now*." He said the baby was ready to be born and he was confident everything would be fine. While he scheduled the OR, I paged my friend and pediatrician Jody. We were both on staff at the hospital and I thought that if she was already there she could come to the OR and be there for the birth. Luckily she was. I watched the entire birth. It was intense and I was anxious to hold Joe. Pete and I knew we were having a baby boy because during one of the routine ultrasounds we had watched him pee. We were so excited! We immediately named him after Pete's father, Joe, who had died of a heart attack when Pete was just 20.

This time Pete said, "Now when you hold him, even if you think he looks like another name, can we agree to stick with 'Joe'?" I agreed, with a smile.

As soon as Joe was born everyone in the room was busy! While the doctor was closing me up Jody suggested that Pete go with her to the next room while the baby was cleaned and weighed and she could examine him. She said they would be right back. "Of course," I said, "but bring that pumpkin back to me as soon as you can." I must have dozed off. When I opened my eyes I was in what seemed like a hallway, but I wasn't sure where I was. A nurse was there and I asked her for my baby. She said that I should rest a little, that it had only been a minute since they took him to weigh him and they would be back soon. This happened a few times and I was thinking that maybe she was confusing me with someone else. I became a little frightened. I did not know where I was, where Pete was, the doctor or Jody. The nurse assured me it had only been minutes; the doctor had given me medication for pain so it had made me drowsy.

"Really, Mrs. Hoagland, relax. I promise they will be here as soon as they are finished. Everything is fine." I looked at the clock. The next time I woke up I looked at the clock again and saw that half an hour had passed. Clearly upset, I began pulling at the IVs.

The nurse rushed to the bed. "Mrs. Hoagland, what do you think you are doing?"

"I have to get out of here and find my baby! Something is not right! Where is my doctor? Where did you take my baby?"

I am not sure if I was given a sedative or what happened, but the next thing I remember is the doctor at my side.

"Deena," he said, "there is a problem with the baby. We are going to send him to the University of Colorado Hospital for a test."

I started crying. "What kind of problem?"

The doctor answered, "It's his heart. We need to check it out and we will know more after some tests are done. You need to get some rest and let us take care of him now."

Still crying, I asked, "Can I see him? Please, can I see him?"

"Yes, I will bring him to you," the doctor said. They brought in the isolette. I had never seen anything like it before. It was made of plastic that you could see through. It had two large holes on both sides; I guessed for the nurse's hands to fit through. I do not remember him looking

different from Kate. He was pink, but bigger than Kate —
almost eight pounds! He was attached to monitors of some
kind. They said they were in a hurry and let me put my hand
in one of the holes. I touched him with my index finger. Then
they whisked him away. Peter was there, his face grim and
worried. He was assuring me that everything would be all
right, that we had the best doctors.

He said, "Jody thinks she heard a heart murmur. It's
important to check it out. I'm sure once they check it out Joe
will be back. Honey, he is big baby; he looks healthy in every
way and his Apgar scores were perfect. Maybe Jody is being
too cautious, but we just need to hang in there and see what
they say."

I was moved to a private room on the maternity floor.
Pete didn't know what to do or where to go. Kate was with
friends at our house in Kittredge. Should he go there? Should
he stay with me? Should he go to the other hospital and wait
in the neonatal intensive care waiting room? They had taken
Joe to the neonatal ICU at the University of Colorado
Hospital. The nurse gave me something she said was for
pain. It knocked me out and I was asleep until the next
morning. Pete went home to be with Kate. In the morning I
was distraught and crazy with emotion. When the nurse
came I asked her what was happening to Joe. She said she
would call the hospital to find out. When she came back she
told me that he was going to have a test — a cardiac
catheterization to diagnose the problem. We would know
something by that afternoon or tomorrow morning at the
latest. I asked her for a breast pump. My milk was coming in

and I was uncomfortable. I thought that I should be saving my milk for Joe.

As the day drew on it became emotionally harder and harder as reality began to sink in. All I could think about was Joe alone in a crib in another hospital. Was anyone holding him? What if he was crying? How would all of this affect our bonding? When Peter came into the room he looked ragged. He had been running between Joe in one hospital, me in another and Kate in the mountains. He did not look like he had gotten any sleep. He said he had made a few calls to his family and to my father and of course to our closest friends. Then we held each other and cried into each other's arms. I think it was the first time that we were ever frightened about something. By the next morning I still had not heard anything about Joe. I decided I felt good enough to get out of bed and walk around.

In the hallway expectant mothers and fathers were walking the halls, trying to get their labor to progress. It wasn't exactly what I needed to see. Looking the other direction I saw people visiting with new parents — happy people all around. Not what I needed to see either. In despair I walked back into my room and decided to put some clothes on. I unhooked the IV, slipped into my clothes, washed my face and decided to go to the University of Colorado Hospital myself. I went down the hall unnoticed and stepped into the elevator. I took my time walking slowly through the lobby and through the revolving doors out to the street. It was a beautiful day. The sun was shining and although it was November it could have been a spring day. As I stepped closer to the curb to ask for a cab, my doctor passed the other way. He waved and I waved back trying to act normal. It was only seconds before it registered and he was upon me.

"What the hell do you think you're doing?" his voice quite stern.

"My baby needs me. He must be really hungry. I have to go to see him!"

"You are not supposed to be out of the hospital yet! You have to go back upstairs."

I began to cry, to fall apart. "I don't even remember what he looks like. I need to hold him in my arms. He needs to know we are there for him. He must be scared and alone. Babies should not be alone!"

"Let's go upstairs," he said. "I will help you figure this out."

Supporting my arm we took the elevator back to the maternity floor and my room. We sat and talked. He was a good friend too. We had known each other for years. This was hard for him he said, but promised we would figure it out.

"Please, give me a few minutes and I will be back," he said.

Once back in my room he had a plan. His secretary Francis would come every few hours and bring my milk to Joe as long as needed. He said I could call Joe's nurse as often as I wanted and he gave me her number in the ICU unit. Francis, he said, would go there right now and bring back a Polaroid photo of Joe.

Three excruciating days later, three doctors entered my room. I felt like I was watching a movie — something not really happening to me, to us. The doctors, wearing khaki pants and tailored shirts with stethoscopes swung around their necks, looked so young and cool — they must be our age! How could what they were saying be true? They were pediatric cardiologists. They told us that Joe was born with an extremely rare heart defect called *truncus arteriosus*, a congenital heart disease in which a single blood vessel comes out of the left and right ventricles, instead of the normal two vessels. In addition, there were several holes between the two ventricles. Beyond that he had two insufficient heart valves and was missing the wall between the lower chambers of his heart. It happens once in one-hundred-thousand births. I couldn't catch my breath. I couldn't hear the full sentences, only intermittent words. The anxiety was overwhelming. I just wanted to know that it could be fixed. "How many children like this have you seen?" I asked. They seemed to dodge the question, or was it my imagination?

"Can I speak to another parent who has had to go through this or something similar?"

They seemed to dodge that one, too.

"It would be a breach of confidentiality," they said.

"Well, how many surgeries have you done here?" This time I was more persistent.

The answer was twelve!

I was thinking, Twelve! . . . "What happened to these twelve children?"

The answer came slowly. I heard that nine of the twelve children died. No one knew where the other three were. Maybe the families had moved. The only thing that I *did* hear clearly was, "Ninety percent mortality."

Oh, my God! It was hard to believe and easy to deny. I cried for what seemed like an endless amount of time. I remember Pete asking, "How long can you keep crying? When will you stop?" *He* was the strong one, the wise one. He had to be. He was running between Kate, at home in the mountains with our friends, and the other hospital where our baby Joe had been taken three days earlier. Pete had to be the one to hold me, make me feel safe again, make me stop and realize that the only things in my control now were to get Joe the best care, and to be the best parents, to help our family.

Pete was right. The longer I cried, the longer Joe would be without us, even if just emotionally on some level. Joe needed us and that was what dried my eyes. It was surreal when we finally took him home just days later, knowing that he was so fragile and sick. He didn't look sick or act sick. Peter was told to go to the hospital where Joe was, as Joe was ready to be discharged. He and Kate picked him up, wrapped in a blanket, and then walked her new baby brother to the hospital where I was — only three blocks away! Kate climbed into bed with me and together we held Joe for the first time. Somehow she had found a Band-Aid and she put it on his little arm. In her own way she knew that her baby brother was sick. In her way she was trying her best to help him too. Kate had been the center of our lives for three years. Not only was a new baby going to be an adjustment for her, but bringing home a sick baby was frightening and more than we could even conceive of.

Hospitals, white coats, grandpa and stethoscopes

When my father arrived he was disheveled and looked like he had not slept well in a long time. He wanted to hold the baby.

"No, you are full of germs!" I said.

I was afraid of everything. He sat in the room reading a newspaper. Then he began to cry softly. I could tell he was crying.

"Dad, why are you crying? I need you to be strong."

He answered softly, between tears, "I should have been the one to go, to die. *She* would have known what to do. What can *I* do for you? I know nothing. I know nothing about this. I am useless here. All I can do is pray, and ask her if she is there to watch over and help us now."

The three doctors came to discharge us: He has *truncus arteriosus*. Here is the medicine. If he spits up call the hospital. (But *every* baby spits up!) No visitors. In six months they will operate on his heart. Three operations they say. See you in six months.

WAIT! STOP! RIGHT NOW . . . STOP!

As I lay in bed, my dreams of our perfect family destroyed, I thought of everything I could to change the situation. I could leave, run away. We could relinquish him. This must be a mistake. I bargained with God. I prayed, but

[50]

nothing changed the reality. Nothing I could think of were *real* options. There was no changing this situation, no running away, and I could never leave. I am a princess, I thought. My father always told me I had nothing to worry about; everything would be good in my life. I was his princess. But I had given up that crown. I had turned it in a long time ago. I am not a princess anymore.

"How long will you cry?" Pete asked. "This baby needs us. I need you. Kate needs you." He was right. I had to stop crying. I had to stop crying. But I was so frightened — frightened to leave the safety of that hospital room. Most of all, frightened of my new reality. This was not how it was supposed to be.

As long as I pretended that everything was okay, I could get along pretty well. There were days when I would trick myself just to get through. I guess I still do that sometimes when the reality of things is too much. I used to think that it was a bad thing to do. But it worked. And sometimes, *just* getting through is all that counts, all you can do.

It took a few days for everything to settle in our minds, to realize this was our new reality. Our baby was sick. Not only was he sick, but he could die. I kept thinking someone was going to knock on the door or call on the phone and tell me that a terrible mistake had been made; that the reports had been switched by accident and that Joe was really fine. It was *another* baby who was sick. But that never happened. During the day we were so busy with both children we had little time to talk about things. At night after they were both asleep we would go around and around about everything we had been learning about *truncus arteriosus*. This was before computers; we did not have the internet or access to a library nearby.

One night we decided to make a list of all the questions we wanted answered. Then Peter had the idea to phone every department of pediatric cardiology in the largest children's hospitals across the country. He began by choosing the biggest cities.

After a few phone calls, when he would say "I am the father of a baby diagnosed with *truncus arteriosus* and would like some information," a very nice person on the other end replied "Sir, if I were you I would try to get in touch with a Doctor E. He is the surgeon who invented a protocol for this diagnosis." The person on the phone thought the doctor had retired from performing surgeries, but knew he was teaching at the University of Chicago. This was great news for us. Peter gathered together his questions and made the call.

When the doctor's secretary answered the phone, Peter simply asked, "Is Paul in please?"

She replied, "Yes. Who should I say is calling?"

Peter said, "Please tell him it is Peter Hoagland." And Dr. E took the call! He was very gracious. After apologizing for the intrusion, Peter told him our story and asked his advice. Doctor E told Peter that he had in fact trained a few surgeons. One he knew was practicing at a hospital in San Francisco and there was another in Boston and one in Texas. He urged Peter to call the other hospitals to ask about the

[52]

mortality rate, the number of nurses staffing the ICU, how many of those held master's degrees, and whether or not it was an ICU reserved solely for cardiac patients. He said that a total of 100 surgeries of this type had already been performed in the U.S. and that there were maybe five surgeons who had experience.

Most importantly, he urged Peter not to wait until Joe was six months old to have his first surgery. He said waiting could be very dangerous. He urged Peter to make the calls sooner rather than later. Peter was grateful for his advice and immediately began to make the phone calls.

Peter and I divided the responsibilities between us. We became a stronger team — a team not willing to lose. After gathering all the information he could, Peter interviewed the five surgeons and all the hospitals in the country with experience operating on patients with *truncus arteriosus*. Dr. E's advice guided Peter through the process of elimination. Peter found the surgeon who had performed the surgery more times than anyone in the world — forty-five operations. The San Francisco hospital where these surgeries took place had an ICU unit just for pediatric cardiac patients and the majority of the nurses held master's degrees. Although his findings were sobering, we both agreed that he had done a spectacular job of finding a solution and that the San Francisco hospital was the best possible option for Joe.

The next steps were difficult ones as we tried to prepare ourselves for what was soon to come. There was no way to truly be prepared; we were entering unknown territory. Despite the situation I think we did the best anyone could. Peter rented an apartment close to the hospital. The hospital social worker told us to be prepared to be there for about six to eight weeks. We decided that we had to bring Kate along. It would be much too difficult to be apart for that long, for her as well as for all of us. Once we arrived in California we would look to hire a nanny to watch her while we were at the hospital with Joe. We had decided that this plan would not be much different than her routine at home. My father said he would meet us in California a few days after our arrival, giving us some time to get settled. We were frightened beyond belief.

The apartment Peter rented was just blocks from the hospital with a beautiful park and botanical garden nearby. We tried to act normal, like we were a "normal" family. We explored the park and our new neighborhood. I am not sure how we looked to the outside world but I can tell you that each of us was fighting our own mental war. We told Kate that we were there to fix Joe's heart. She seemed to accept everything in stride. She was happy to read her storybooks and play with her toys in the waiting rooms. Peter and I took turns with the children so that we each had time with both. Kate would watch the children in the hallways walking with their IV poles and when she had questions we answered them as honestly as we could. We decided we never wanted to lie to her as that might cause her more anxiety and make her distrust us. Our policy was to answer her questions as honestly as possible and give her only the information that she asked for — nothing more.

When Joe was admitted to the hospital I met with the nurse alone while Pete was with Kate. She asked if I understood the reason for the hospitalization. "Yes," I answered. When she asked how she could be of help, I asked if there was a sibling program or a nanny referral service. She explained that this was a hospital and she did not have any information or know of any programs like that for siblings. She explained she was only there to answer questions about the surgery or the hospital. So we spoke about the surgery and all of its procedures. I asked for a tour of the ICU. I wanted to be prepared for what I would see. I was already feeling overwhelmed by everything on the surgical floor. But she said that only the immediate families of current ICU patients were allowed in and that we would learn everything we needed to know in the next few days. I could feel my throat closing, my heart pounding loudly. I was actually surprised she didn't hear it as well. She showed me the breast pump room where I would be spending a lot of time over the next few weeks. I was surprised at how dim and uninviting it all was.

"What was I expecting?" I thought to myself.

I was already telling myself if I were the director of this hospital I'd make this room look more like a family den than a storage room! The waiting room was full. The television on the wall was blaring. A soap opera was on. The room was crowded but not one person was watching the television. So why was it on? They all looked like they had been there too long. No one looked at one another.

The nurse showed me what would be our room. When we were done I commented that the people in the waiting room looked worn out. She told me that many of them had very sick children and had been there for weeks on end.

"That is so sad," I said. "I feel so fortunate that I am not in that situation and that we will be going home soon. It must be hard to work here and always see such sick children. All the rooms are filled!" They looked so sick — it was so sad.

She looked at me with a puzzled expression.

I guess I was looking for reassurance when I said that, but instead she replied, "Mrs. Hoagland I do hope for you and your family's sake that you will be going home soon, but I would not plan on that. Joe is the sickest baby on this floor."

I was stunned. Her words played over and over in my head as if she had spoken a foreign language and I was left trying to decipher what she had just said. Then she smiled and kindly excused herself. Our room was the one next to the nurses' station.

The girl in the next bed

Walking down the hall I tried my best to keep my eyes forward. I am not going to tell Pete what she said, I thought. I wondered if there were things he might know that he was keeping from *me*? I thought about asking him but realized I was feeling as though I knew all that I was capable of knowing at that moment. If I needed or wanted to know more I would ask him then. It was hard not to look into the rooms where the doors were opened. The place smelled antiseptic; everything clean. Everyone walks down the hall trying hard not to look. It was Charlie, the janitor, who held my gaze and smiled. He has eyes that see too much, I thought. He knows what's going on here. We were checking in to the "No Hope Hotel," the place you go when your pediatrician says here-are-the-names-of-the-best-in-the-country-call-them-and-see-what-they-have-to-say.

Our hospital room was large. There were four beds separated by curtains to provide a sense of privacy. There was a metal crib for Joe and lots of machines and wires. The sounds were overwhelming and I wondered how the babies could ever sleep, get rest and grow in here? I tried hard to smile and look at the nurse when she spoke to me. I don't really know what I was looking at. I remember telling myself to look as though I understood what she was saying and to smile when she smiled at me. And to breathe. Just breathe. I had to remind myself to breathe.

I did ask a few questions and I know I answered all of hers. Outwardly I must have looked calm, but inside I was petrified, in shock, and wondering how it was possible to be split in two like this — able to carry on but breaking down inside, living one breath at a time. Pete was with Kate seeing the sights of San Francisco and trying to stay busy. I was alone with Joe. I longed for my mother. The babies in the next beds were asleep I imagined, because they were not making any sounds. All I could see were people's shoes beneath the curtains.

I sat in a rocking chair next to Joe's crib and held him in my arms while he slept. He was eight weeks old and so beautiful, so perfect. It was impossible to imagine that there was anything wrong with him or that he had to have open-heart surgery. He had no symptoms at all. I was still hoping someone would walk in and tell me there was a big mistake and call it all off. The room grew dark as I sat in the rocking chair watching my beautiful baby boy sleep. This could be our last night together, I thought. The reality of it was indescribable. I wept softly so no one could hear me. I asked God to help us through this, to save my baby boy and give us the strength we needed. Please, God. Please, God. Are you there?

All night long the woman behind the curtain at the next crib sang softly to her baby. I thought she sounded at ease and I wondered how anyone could be at ease in this situation. I wished I could be like her, confident and softly singing to my beautiful baby. Soon they would come for him and I would have to hand him over.

Morning came and so did the nurses to prepare Joe for surgery. It was quick; they must plan it that way. I kissed him goodbye and as they wheeled his little crib away, I sat in the rocking chair waiting for Pete and cried. He would be there as soon as he could. When Kate woke up he would feed her breakfast and they would come right over. The crying came as if the flood gates had opened and I could no longer hide it.

The other mom behind the curtain came to me and said, "I can't help but hear you crying. I wanted to come to you in the night but I was not sure I should. Instead I sang."

"Your singing was lovely," I said, choking on my tears.

She told me her daughter had undergone many open-heart surgeries and she remembered how especially

[58]

frightened she had been during the first one. I told her I was worried about the scar. She invited me to see her daughter's. I thought it would help to see a child alive and well who had been through the surgery too. She pulled the curtain so I could see her daughter. I had difficulty standing, breathing. Lying in the crib was a deformed child in a vegetative state. The child was attached to every possible monitor. As she lay there not moving I could not move as well. I have remembered this mother and this child for all these years. I saw the scar — the least of her worries. I walked the halls in shock at the No Hope Hotel. The only eyes I searched for at that moment were the knowing eyes of the janitor named Charlie, hoping his kind eyes could guide me to the waiting room where I would find the comfort of Peter, Kate and my father.

We waited for about five hours, which seemed like a lifetime, before they came to talk to us. The surgery was a success! What a relief! Joe would be brought up from recovery soon. He would go to the ICU and stay there until he was deemed stable enough to go back to a room on the surgical floor. I felt myself breathe. I felt a tiny sense of "normal" for the first time in two months. When they finally allowed us to see Joe, he was still heavily sedated. The doctors said he would be this way for a long time so as to remain still, to rest and recover slowly. There were monitors and tubes everywhere. He had one large tube coming from his mouth enabling him to get oxygen, as he was not breathing on his own. "Intubated" they called it.

Everywhere I looked he was wired to something. He was resting, the nurse said, and we were only allowed in the ICU for ten minutes at a time. The nurse encouraged us to get something to eat. She said that she would be with him through the night and asked for our phone number in case she needed to reach us. We decided we would get dinner and then check on Joe one more time before going back to the apartment to sleep for the night. I was numb with exhaustion. We had found a great seafood place right around the corner from the apartment that had quickly become our favorite neighborhood hangout. The bartender noticed us as soon as we walked in and asked, "Where is that cute baby you had with you before?" We told him a bit about Joe. He was kind to ask and to listen and sent drinks to the table on the house. "I am sure you both could use these right now." he said. When I put my head on the pillow that night I could have slept for a week! I never heard my father sneak out in the night to go to the hospital. Neither did Pete.

In the morning we ate as fast as we could and went straight to the ICU. There was my father asleep in the rocking chair next to Joe's crib. The nurse said he had come in at about midnight. She said it was a quiet night and when Dad fell asleep she did not have the heart to wake him and tell him he had to leave. She let him stay there all night. Joe was doing well she said, stable as expected. We were so happy!

We sat in the waiting room most of the day taking turns going in to see Joe and taking walks with Kate. Dad said that since Joe was doing so well and was on his way to recovery he planned to go home. In the afternoon he went to see Joe and say a special prayer for him before taking a cab to the airport. When we hugged goodbye he said, "Don't you worry, *mamala*. God is listening to me and everything will be all right."

"Thanks, Dad," I said, wishing I had his faith.

We had friends from college living in San Francisco who came to visit us that afternoon. They took Kate with them for the rest of the day so we could focus on Joe. We planned to get Kate later that evening and meet them for dinner. When we went in to the ICU at around 4:00 pm we noticed that Joe was looking very chubby. I was thinking he looked like he might have the facial features of a child with Down syndrome. I was confused. Nobody had said anything to me before about him having Down syndrome, but it was obvious to me that he had those facial features now. I asked the nurse, "Why didn't anyone tell us that Joe had Down syndrome?"

The nurse answered quietly, "Joe does look like that doesn't he? But that is not the problem."

"What is the problem then?" I asked feeling dizzy and faint now. She said she would call the doctors and have them explain. She would send them to the waiting room to find us shortly. In the waiting room Peter and I could not speak. We were tense. It seemed like an hour before the doctor came. He said that Joe was retaining fluids. "I don't know why. We've checked everything. There is one more test we are going to run, and if that does not give us any clues I'm afraid to say it does not look good right now." He then added,

"Please don't leave. Joe may only have about an hour unless we can figure out the problem."

We saw a large machine being wheeled into the ICU. "That is the echocardiogram for Joe. I will come back when I have some news," he said. That next hour was unbearable. I looked at the clock every few minutes. I realized that if I could get through five minutes then I could get through ten. If I could get through ten minutes then I could get through another five. Just breathing. That is how I survived until the doctor returned. This time he walked into the waiting room with confidence and explained that the IV lines into Joe's pericardium that were supposed to be bringing him the medications he needed had not been reaching him. "We saw this on the echo. The lines must have gotten pulled out of place somehow and we replaced them. He is getting the medication he needs and we will know in a short time if this is going to do the trick and get him back on board."

We waited to hear that Joe was turning the corner and doing well again. That night Peter stayed in the waiting room outside the ICU and checked on Joe every few hours throughout the night. We took turns for the next 21 days knowing we could not leave him alone. By the time Joe was ready to be discharged, I had pumped enough breast milk to fill a giant cooler! I tried to donate it to the hospital thinking there would be another baby who could use it, but because the hospital couldn't take the time to test for HIV and other possible transmittable diseases they turned down the offer. I told Pete, "This milk is gold!" I had worked too hard to get it to see it poured down a drain, so we bought a cooler, packed it with dry ice and took it all home!

We had made many friends at the hospital and in our little corner of San Francisco. We were happy and so thankful to be leaving the No Hope Hotel and going home to our mountaintop — home to what I had once thought of as our "normal" life.

The canyon drive

Coming home to Kittredge and our beautiful mountain was a victory! It felt so good to be back in our own beds. After a short recovery time, life should be normal again. The doctors said everything went well. They said when Joe turns six we can do the surgery again and then again when he turns 18. Okay. I thought we would be okay.

It was winter, with cold and snowy days, but life was coming around. Then Joe caught a cold. It quickly turned serious and he struggled to breathe and move. He began to look pale, bluish and gray. I called the doctors every day asking for help. When I brought him to the pediatrician she said that it was just a cold; he would be fine. So back up the mountain I would go, feeling crazy. Why can't they see he is not moving? Why are they not doing something to help him? Finally, the pediatrician decided to come to our house. It was then that she saw how serious his condition had become and ordered the oxygen that Joe would require 24 hours a day. The oxygen tube had to be taped in place and his little face was beginning to get sore from the taping. She wondered if the high altitude might be what's been causing him distress.

Whenever he delivered oxygen, the respiratory therapist would stay and chat a bit. He was my only friend those days. It was he who found me crying. It was during one of his deliveries that he said to me, "Mrs. Hoagland, if I did not know better I would say Joe acts like he has a hole in his heart. But I know that his heart has been fixed already." All day and night I could not get his words out of my head. In the morning I phoned the cardiologist in Denver. Exasperated with me he phoned Peter and told him I was driving them crazy with my calls. He said there was no need for all of this concern; that Joe was nursing and sleeping and growing as he should be. That night Peter told me I was crazy. Maybe I had postpartum blues. Maybe I should see a therapist myself. He told me to stop calling the doctors. I was so hurt, but thought I had to do something — anything! I could not let things go on this way. I called Joe's cardiologist and told him I was going to visit my father, who had moved to Florida. I asked if they would make an exception and do Joe's follow-up cardiac test early so that we could stay in Florida for the rest of the winter.

"Sure," he said. "How about tomorrow?"

That's just what I wanted, I thought. Now Joe can have the test and I can get it off my mind. If there's nothing wrong, I'll go to therapy. But if there *is* something wrong we can fix it. In the morning we went into Denver for the test. Peter and I sat quietly in the waiting room. The entire time I was waiting I was telling myself how ridiculous I had been driving everyone crazy, thinking Joe was sick. I needed help. They were right. I thought. I must have postpartum

[64]

depression. After all, look at all we had been through. If I don't go talk to someone I'll lose my friends and my husband.

Finally, in they walked, all three doctors, wearing their starched white coats and stethoscopes around their necks. They were walking briskly down the hall toward us. Okay, I can take it, I thought. I would make a counseling appointment for myself as soon as we got home.

They stood in front of us and began, "Mrs. Hoagland, we owe you an apology."

What? Why? What are you saying? Oh no, I owe you an apology! I should not have bothered you so much, I was thinking. What are they saying? Try to listen, try to listen.

"Joe has another hole."

I could not grasp everything they were saying right away. There I go again trying so hard to listen to words I do not want to be hearing. Our surgeon had already been notified in San Francisco. It was okay to fly with Joe on commercial air. Joe's second open-heart surgery had been scheduled for the next day. What? Another open-heart surgery! This is an emergency! Oh, my God. Oh, God, help us now. Please, God, answer the phone!

On our way back up the canyon, Peter apologized for doubting me. He said, "We will get through this, you'll see. We have the best doctors in the world. We have all the resources." I heard his words and tried so hard to believe him. Oh, God, help us now. Guide us. Be there for us now.

The suitcases came out again. In went some clothes, Kate's favorite toys and books. Hurry! We must hurry! "Kate, you need to listen to mama now. We all have to go and help baby Joe again in San Francisco." Bewildered, she followed along as any three-year-old would.

Loading the car I told Gerda, our nanny, that I hoped we would be back. She asked me what I was talking about. "Why are you talking this way?" But there are times when I *know* things. I can't explain it. Somehow I just knew, at that moment, that Colorado was over. Driving down the canyon to the airport everything seemed to move in slow motion. The water in the creek running over the rocks glistened as I observed each droplet — the leaves in the trees, the birds, the great big blue sky with the perfect clouds, the Colorado that I loved, all in slow motion, as if I was saying goodbye to each and every particle. I could not talk. Remember to breathe, I thought. Please, God, help me, help us now! God, where are you today? Can you hear me? Can you see me?

Back at the No Hope Hotel, I hate it that I know where things are — that I am familiar with this place. The people, the nurses all look happy to see us. They are our friends and some even feel like family, at the No Hope Hotel, the club where I would never want to be accepted. The club I never wanted to join wants me as a lifetime member! Ugh!

The doctors run tests and find three holes in Joe's heart. Because of the high altitude, his cold ripped open the sutures that had been so carefully placed. At their rounds the next morning our room is crowded with residents, interns and doctors — more than we had ever seen. They are talking to one another as if we are not in the room. "The mother said . . . The child is . . ."

[66]

But I *am* here! *Yoo-hoo*! They want to see if he can gain weight. Joe is fragile, too frail to operate on right now. The surgery was canceled. He wouldn't survive it.

Having rented an apartment just blocks from the hospital, we decided to stay in California a month to see if living at sea level would help Joe gain weight. The waiting was hard but we passed the time by taking walks in Golden Gate Park, touring the chocolate factory and visiting with old high-school and college friends. We did everything we could think of to fatten up Joe, because that's what the doctors wanted. The nurses had given us supplements that added extra calories to my milk. At the end of our month we were anxiously hoping for good news at our next doctor's visit. Although Joe had gained a little weight, it wasn't enough. Now that they had identified altitude as the problem, they wanted to see if he could gain some more.

Our friends Joe and Cynthia talked us into moving in with them. We loved them. Looking back, I am amazed that they were so willing and gracious to take us in and take us on. They were working and we definitely were an invasion of their privacy. We were so grateful for this time with them and I'm not sure we would have made it without their support.

By our next visit to the doctor, Joe had gained a little more weight but was still quite fragile. Feeling like we were visitors who smelled like bad fish after three days, Peter decided we should fly to Florida and stay with my father in Palm Beach. By now we were feeling the financial strain as well. After a few weeks at Dad's it was evident that his condo was too small for all of us to stay in, so Peter called his uncle in Tequesta. Uncle Ray and his wife Trudy were in real estate. They said Pete could work for them and they would help us find a furnished rental house. At least then we could be in a place of our own. It had been almost one year since Joe was born and we had never stopped running for his next breath.

That winter, after we settled into an old ranch house just blocks from the beach, Pete returned to our house in Colorado because he was afraid the pipes would freeze. I was afraid he was slowly making his exit from us. Why should he want to stay? I became depressed. We had a dying baby, we both hated Florida, and all of our friends and our life were back on the mountain with everything else that he loved — friends, fishing and skiing.

For several months, it became necessary for Peter to travel back and forth, every three weeks or so, between Florida and Colorado. During his absence I did my best to take care of everything alone. By the time summer arrived, it had become unbearably hot outside — so hot that I thought an egg could fry if it landed on my forehead. On those days, the doctors didn't want Joe going outside during the day. They said his heart would have to work too hard. So I would wait inside until the late afternoon sun was about to go down. Kate, Joe, the dogs and I would hurry down the street to the beach. We would walk at the ocean's edge until we were too tired to walk anymore. Joe was always in the backpack and Kate just steps ahead, chasing the birds, the ocean, and collecting shells. This was my favorite time. People would often come up to talk. They would tell me how beautiful the children were.

Kate loved it when the turtles came to nest. She loved it even more when the turtle eggs hatched. We became turtle midwives that summer, helping the babies crawl out of the footprints in which they became stuck.

There was an old man who seemed to be about my father's age who walked the beach every night too. He walked with a golf club, a putter, as one would use a walking stick. He was always alone when he walked. I knew he was watching us. I could see him looking, and I was sure he was curious about us, as we were new to the beach and we were there every night. I wondered if he was asking himself, Where was the daddy? Why was this woman always alone with her children and the dogs?

Night after night we walked the beach. One night he approached and asked about the dogs. He thought they were so much fun and unusual looking. Asta was a Sussex spaniel. She was the sweetest dog, all chocolate brown, with a long body like a Labrador and a big Lab head, but with springer spaniel hair and ears. Most people have never seen a dog like her. She was different. Her eyes were soulful and she ran with a bit of a spring and a hop. He asked me about the children and whether I was alone, if I had a husband, and why I walked the beach at night and why we never came out during the day? He lived nearby, he said, and had noticed all of these things about us. I shared our story.

[69]

After that, we met almost every night and walked the beach together. He was great company to me even when we did not talk much. Most days he was the only person I spoke with, other than the children.

It wasn't until months later that I found out from a neighbor that my beach friend was Perry Como! He lived in the neighborhood and kept mostly to himself, so this neighbor was intrigued that we were walking partners. That intrigued me too. I never let him know that I knew who he was, assuming if he wanted me to know he would have told me. I was also afraid that he might not walk with me anymore if I said anything about it, so I never asked him about himself. We would talk about the ocean, the turtles, the birds, that night's sunset — just easy, nothing talk. I loved this time and looked forward to it every evening. Although I knew the changing tides could never wash away my worries, they did lighten my load, if only for an hour. It was an hour that I cherished.

In the back of my mind I kept thinking Peter was waiting for a time when Joe was well and things were stable to tell me that he wanted to go back to Colorado to live. It wasn't that I thought he didn't love us, but I could see him struggling to find his way. He had no friends in Florida. How do you make new friends when your life is in chaos? There was nothing besides us bringing him back or keeping him in Florida. After all, why would we stay there if we didn't have to? We missed everything about our mountain life. I certainly understood those feelings. I knew he craved fishing and skiing and being with his friends. I knew he was missing "normal," whatever that was. He was going back and forth between working in Colorado and visiting us in Florida and was under so much stress trying to keep our lives together when it was torn into so many pieces.

Whenever Peter came to visit I became more and more aware of the strain on our life. Never before had we needed to work so hard at just being together, searching for whatever happiness we could find, as if it was a lost treasure, with no map to guide us. I began to think that Peter was distancing himself from Joe. Maybe it was easier for him to do that so he wouldn't feel the pain. But it was hard for me to watch. He did not pick him up, cuddle or interact with him as he had done with Kate when she was a baby. This was really hard for me, not only because I felt like I was doing everything for Joe and needed a little break; but I began to worry about the distance that might come between all of us if Peter was really doing this. It was during one of his trips to Florida that I told him I had a bad headache and that he needed to put the kids to bed. I went to our bedroom to lie down. For over an hour I had not heard one sound coming from the room where the kids were sleeping. I knew they had to be asleep by now so I went looking for Peter. I found him sitting on the floor in the dark room with Joe still in his arms. Joe was fast asleep.

As I quietly approached, Peter's eyes met mine. Tears streaming down his face, holding Joe, looking up at me he said, "He's the best little boy. He's our little fighter, Deens. He's so sick."

We held each other and cried and cried until there were no more tears to cry. I told Peter that night how I feared he would set me up in Florida and leave us there to go live in Colorado. I told him I would understand if he did. I told him I thought he had been distancing himself to make it easier for him to do so.

He said, "I love you. I could never leave you or the kids. I would never do anything like that!"

Maybe he *had* been distancing himself a little, but that was the only way he knew how to deal with things. He was having an equally difficult time dealing with all of the changes and losses in his life. Of course he was. We had so much going on that there had hardly been a moment to talk through our thoughts, fears and anxieties. Whenever we did have the time, neither one of us wanted to spend those precious moments talking about the things that had gone wrong in our life.

Peter and I felt everything was spinning out of control. How could we not? It was time to stop feeling like victims and start finding the power we didn't even know we had. We decided that night that with our future truly unknown, for all of our sakes, we would do everything we could to make sure the moments we had together counted. If Joe doesn't make it through this, we have to be able to look back and say we did everything that we possibly could. Eventually we would have to be able to say to ourselves that no matter what the circumstances, we hadn't failed, for better or worse. Isn't that what we promise one another and ourselves, to find a way to see it through the good times *and* the bad? Somehow, that night, we embraced the attitude that it was easy to navigate through life's still waters, but it's by navigating through the storms that we find our true strength. Sometimes the only thing that kept us going was hope. So instead of counting my breaths, I began counting my blessings.

That night it felt to us that we had married each other again. We discovered an even stronger love between us, something far beyond what most people can understand, realizing this commitment required greater determination than either of us had ever expected. Someone once asked me how we got through those days. I know that it was our love that carried us. I also know that I spent a lot of time pretending, too — pretending that everything was all right.

We returned to California every three weeks so that the cardiologists and surgeons could check Joe's heart and see if he was strong enough to withstand another surgery. Joe was eleven months old when they said it was time for them to perform the surgical repair. Back to San Francisco and the hospital we went. Peter's mother and sister came to Florida and Kate stayed with them. This time we believed she would be better off staying home with family and keeping the routine that she had become used to. She was attending preschool and had some friends to keep her busy. I had never been apart from her for that long and was sad to leave her behind, but we knew that this plan was probably the best for her. I was worried about Joe not surviving this surgery. How would we deal with it? How could we ever explain it to Kate? My brain hurt from thinking and worrying. We left for San Francisco.

By now most people at the hospital knew us on a first-name basis. I was no longer wearing pumps and pearls. I looked like the rest of the people in the waiting room, with that worn-down, too-much-coffee, not enough sleep, money, or laughter to-get-me-through-the-day look. Such is life in the No Hope Hotel. I now, too, tried hard not to look too deeply into the eyes of others — to know their stories was to know more pain and there was no more room in my heart for any of that.

We were back in that same room with the four beds and curtains. We rented an apartment at the Stanyon Park Hotel. It was frightening how familiar and comfortable everything was. Everywhere we went the acquaintances we had met from the times before remembered us, and especially Joe. Everyone — the janitor, the doorman, the hotel clerks, maids, even the bartender at PJ's Oyster Bar — asked how Joe was doing. It amazed us to realize there were so many people who had been watching us and knew our story without us ever having to tell them — they just knew.

The surgery went well. For the very first time since Joe had been born, we felt relieved and hopeful. It was obvious to both of us that we were not going back to Colorado to live. Once the doctors told us Joe was clear to transfer out of the ICU, Pete made his plans to fly back to Florida to be with Kate. Joe and I would follow in a few days when he was strong enough to make the trip. Pete left for the airport and I realized I was now all alone with Joe.

While he was in the ICU, I slept in the hotel, but as soon as he was moved to the surgical floor I would stay in his room with him. Just hours after Pete was gone something went wrong. The nurses came running. I panicked. Joe's left lung had collapsed! Joe and I spent the next eight weeks together in the hospital. This was an interesting time for me. I learned a lot about myself in those weeks. Mostly that I was strong and smart, and could do anything I needed to do — and I *did* it. I realized then that I was not dependent on anyone, not even Pete. That was the most important part for me: I did not need to be with Pete to survive. I knew I loved him and wanted to be with him. Somehow that freed me to know that no matter what happened, I would find my way and be all right.

In the room with the four beds and the curtains a baby slept across from Joe. He was very frail. His mother was young. She looked the same as I had looked that first day and night one year ago. I couldn't help but overhear the nurses and doctors during their rounds. This baby was critically ill and none of them had much hope for his life. They were not saying it straight like that. They were using the big doctor words, the words I had come to understand.

One year ago it was a new language in a new country, but now I knew enough to understand this baby's story was not a good one. They were talking about putting a band in his

[75]

heart to help him be comfortable. What I understood was they could not repair his heart. I heard them say the procedure would help keep him comfortable until the end, which was not expected to be too much longer.

When the nurses and doctors were gone and we were alone I reached out to her and asked if I could be of any help. Oh, how my heart ached for her. She really had no idea what was happening to her or her baby and he was so sick. I knew this baby was not going to live from what I had overheard. She did not know. She was hopeful. She believed God and the doctors would save her son. I could tell that she and her husband were not close. I could see that they were not a team. She talked a lot about her life and family. She had no one to help her, having been a foster child her entire life. She met her husband in church at a singles group. He was older and had promised to love her and take care of her. They married soon after meeting and she became pregnant almost immediately. Now they had a little boy who was frail and very sick. Her husband blamed her, saying the baby's bad heart must have come from her side of the family, and she accepted that blame. She had known no other way to live than as a victim.

I listened and listened for days. She was convinced that her baby's sickness was her fault. He was taken to the intensive care unit, but Joe and I remained in the room. Between visits to her son, she would come to talk with me instead of sitting alone in the waiting room. I was acquainted with many of the nurses by now, so one day when the nurse and I were alone I begged the nurse to tell her that her baby's heart problem was not genetic. At least, I thought, she could lighten her load and help her stop feeling guilty. It was at that moment that I realized that I was the "regular" on the floor.

That first day, one year ago, when I thought I was going home and would never be like the rest of the people in the waiting room, that nurse had been right to tell me otherwise. I was now a full-fledged member of the club I never intended to join. In fact, I might have just been elected chairman, oblivious that the election had even happened! When the young mother found me the next day I helped her with the laundry room, the breast pump room, and showed her where things were that she would need. I suggested she play music for the baby that she played at home to drown out the beeps of the hospital monitors; keep her photo in his crib so if he opened his eyes and she was not there he could see her image. I told her everything that I had learned over the past year with the hope that she would be empowered and also find her inner strength. She would need every ounce of it.

During those eight weeks Joe seemed to gain strength each day. Everyone on the floor adored him. The nurses would vie to watch over him. I thought it must be because he was getting well. Certainly it must feel better to take care of a child that was going to get better and go home. Joe and I had made many friends over those weeks. The janitor came daily to check on us. The clerks from the hotel would visit often, bringing food and offering to do my laundry. I realized I was not alone. I felt fortunate to learn that there is so much kindness in the world. To learn that kindness like that which I had never known could come from total strangers.

When we finally left the hospital to return to Florida, Joe and I were *both* a lot stronger. I was so happy to go home and join the world again. So many thoughts, images of people's faces, sounds of babies crying, the smells of those weeks on the surgical floor flood my mind even today. I think about the people we met. I don't know what happened to them. I stayed in touch with the nurses and doctors, of course, because of Joe. But the other children and their stories haunt me still. Sometimes I think I want to know, but I don't want to know either. It was all too painful to look at in that moment with everything that we were going through. I wasn't strong enough to stay in touch with them, nor did I have the energy to take on one more thing in my day.

It was during our next hospitalization that a nurse confided in me that one of the mothers wanted to talk to me, to thank me for the things I had helped her with. In my heart I knew who she was right away. We tried to connect by phone a few times and left messages back and forth, but we never did actually speak to each other directly.

◊ ◊ ◊

What followed were three more years of hospitalizations, medications and trips to the doctors. I guess, in the end, the thing that allowed us hope was the fact that the doctors kept telling us that, although Joe had a

[78]

terrible heart defect, it was one they thought could be fixed. And as long as it was fixable, we had hope. We never did go back to Colorado as a family. Realizing we were never going to be able to live on our mountaintop again, we sold those dreams and bought a house in Jupiter, Florida, not far from my dad.

Blue hair and science fiction cockroaches

"I'm afraid I will wake up one day and have blue hair!" I told a Colorado friend on the phone one day. "I will know then something has really gone wrong. And there's a science-fiction-sized cockroach in the corner! What am I doing in this god-forsaken place? I hate Florida! But where would I go? Why would Peter want to stay here? I can't really figure that out."

Pete had said that if we had to be at sea level, then he wanted to be where he could swim, surf and fish, and to be near my father. Dad was 84 now and why not be close to him for this next part of his life?

Izod shirts and khaki shorts

It is hard to look back and tell you about everything that happened then. Hard because it hurt so much, but also because it's in the past and I have learned to put the past right where it belongs: OVER!

Florida was a difficult transition. We were used to the mountains, having no neighbors and the only sounds those of the woods and the wildlife. In Jupiter I kept the windows closed and the air conditioning on. People always asked why. And to me they were crazy to wear sweaters — I was so hot! People all looked the same in Florida. Old women dyed their hair *blue*! What's that about? I still do not get that. Old men wore white shoes. Even though it was 1990 they were still dressing in leisure suits! Everyone my age wore khaki shorts and Izod shirts. They all looked the same! If a child was lost and little they might grab the closest pair of legs, look up and *hope* it was their mommy! I tried to be different, not because I didn't like Floridians, but because I could not easily blend into their world and their way of living. I suppose I was rebelling a little, too. I did not want *this* life. I wanted MY LIFE — whatever that used to be. I was used to being my own person. I had a career (or at least I used to have one, once upon a time). I was spending my days keeping house. I mean, cleaning it *every* day! I had never done that before in my entire life! I hate to clean. But I had to pass the time, and sitting and thinking about anything was the last thing I needed to do.

Since Joe's last hospitalization he had to have a breathing treatment every two hours around the clock. The medicines were overwhelming. I would find myself in front of the medicine cabinet, syringe in hand and bottle on the counter, not remembering whether I was getting it out to give him his medicines or putting them away after having given them to him. I was exhausted and there was no one to call for help. Peter tried to work, but we were both so tired and depressed it was all we could do to hang on hoping that one day we would wake up to a better day. Slowly that happened. Eventually Joe seemed to be growing and doing better. I even enrolled him in a small Montessori preschool. By then Kate was in kindergarten and enrolled in a dance class, which she loved. She had made some good friends and enjoyed her play dates. Things were finally looking up for us.

In spite of all his troubles, Joe was a happy and easygoing little guy. A very funny personality was emerging. He became intrigued with flushing his Lego Duplos down the toilet. Poor Peter! It seemed every week he would have to take the toilet apart to repair it. My father loved having us in Florida and would visit us daily. Joe's visits to the doctor came every six months now. I felt like we had graduated. And then, things changed again.

Pete took a job in Florida City, two hours from where we were living, managing a fish farm. His stepfather had asked him to help out as he had invested in this farm. When Peter got there he called me and said, "This is a wild place, Deens. I love it here! I think you would too."

I was worried about picking up and moving again, especially for Kate's sake. It seemed like we were all just settling in, making some friends and she was enjoying her school. We decided it would be better not to move right away and we would still have to sell the house. Peter and I hated the idea of being apart again but we did not want to uproot the family either, at least not until we knew for sure that this would be a good job and a career that he really wanted. So for the next nine months we lived apart during the week while Peter went to work at the farm. He came home every weekend with stories about alligators, panthers and a wild part of Florida that none of us knew existed. It was exciting and reminded me of our mountain life in Colorado. Living in a suburban neighborhood was not my style. We all missed Peter so much during the week. We listed the house for sale but it seemed that no one wanted to buy it. But when summer came and Kate's school let out, we began thinking that we should go ahead and move to the Keys. We all hated living apart and we needed to be together as a family. It was too hard on all of us having Peter only on the weekends. Kate could begin the new school year without disruption and we would all have a fresh start.

We loved visiting Peter at the fish farm. He was really happy at his job and he was making friends too. Joe loved to fish and to follow his dad around doing "boy" things. Finally we found a house in Key Largo, just 40 minutes from where Peter was working. It was on the ocean with a great yard for the children and the dogs. The house needed a ton of work, but it was the best house for us. For the first time since Joe was born, life was feeling like it was coming together. It had been a long time since we felt like we were a "normal' family!

The long hallway

Three weeks before Joe's next check-up and I wasn't sleeping well, waking every hour to look at the clock. The deep sighs that I don't hear anymore, Pete hears. He does not have to ask what I am thinking. He too feels the impending dread of the hallways and waiting rooms. Dr. G and I are now good friends. He looks into my eyes, understanding my

[82]

anxiety and fear, and asks if I want a Xanax. He is always confused when I turn him down. Joe is almost three now.

We feel confident. It's been 18 months since Joe's last surgery and to us he seems healthy and full of energy. Joe is due for a routine checkup; we aren't going back because of any specific problem. In our minds, the checkups are just something we have to do for the next six years or so until the doctor tells us Joe has to have another surgery. We know he will have to have one more. The doctors had already told us that. But Dr. G explained carefully and slowly that the time to repair Joe's heart is when he is strong so he can withstand the surgery. Dr. G tells us that the last repair just patched the holes caused by Colorado's high altitude. Now he says it's time to change the conduit, the donor tissue that had been implanted to provide a working valve for his heart. He tells us that once this is done we will be back on track with the *truncus* protocol, and reminds us that the altitude had presented an unusual set of circumstances which had set us off course.

It is so difficult for me to look at Joe and see him as sick, now that he is running and playing just like all the other little three-year-olds. Why? I can't wrap my heart and head around this, but I know that the doctors know what's best. Feeling strong now, understanding the hospital, knowing people in San Francisco, we decide this time we can go there brave and confident, having faced the worst already.

Dr. G assures us that this is the right time and so he scheduled Joe's third open-heart surgery. So, back out to California we go. Because it's summer, Kate goes to stay with

[83]

her "Grandma Oma," as Pete's mother was called, so that we can spend our time helping Joe. We tell the kids we are going to go get Joe's heart fixed once and for all, and that when we come back we'll make the move to Key Largo and begin afresh. It will be the perfect way to begin again in a new school and a new place to live that we will all love so much.

Walking down the hall is easier now. I know many people and actually have friends in the hospital and in San Francisco. The janitor, the nurses, and our friends from high school and college come to visit us. This time we rent a room in a funky bed and breakfast in the Haight-Ashbury district, just blocks away from the hospital. It is less expensive than the apartment and we do not need so many rooms as before. We decide that the night before Joe's surgery I will stay with Joe and that once he is in the ICU we will stay in our lovely Japanese Tea Garden Room at the B&B. As soon as Joe is moved to his room, Pete will return home to Kate. It all seems like the perfect plan.

My father joins us in California. He is always with us now. He loves the kids so much and I find his prayers comforting. He and Pete have become really great friends. It is hard watching my father get old. He talks about my mother a lot. It was not so long ago that I found him standing in her closet, everything still in its place just as it had been the day she died. "I can still smell her," he said. "When I come in here I can still smell her. Oh, I wish she were still here! I miss her desperately."

He is such a cute old guy, the widows he knows are all chasing after him. He calls them "barracudas!" His stories of their antics keep our minds busy and make us laugh. I am reminded of how lucky we are to have him in our lives still. Peter made a great decision when he moved us to Florida. Otherwise, we would have never had the chance to know my father this way.

When the surgeon comes to find us he is glowing and proud. They have patched the remaining holes and even performed some cutting-edge thing he is so proud of. He tells us he didn't replace the conduit after all, because he was able to patch it, reducing the time required on the heart-lung machine.

He beams, "The surgery went great! I couldn't be more pleased!"

We are so relieved. By the end of the day the nurses are so happy with Joe's stability that they decide to move him to a regular room! We are ecstatic and overcome with joy! I go back to the B&B to get some rest while Pete stays with Joe for the night in his room. I finally get some sleep, able to rest knowing this worst part is over. Even though we told Dad to go get some rest he always stayed close by for Joe. It was useless to tell him to do otherwise.

Asleep in a puddle of tears, friends are family

Back at the B&B I fell asleep feeling grateful that our life would finally find some normalcy. It was still dark when

[85]

the phone rang. I can't remember answering it and knowing that it was actually the phone — then Peter's voice, but unfamiliar. What was he saying? I was confused. He said, "Come quickly. Something is wrong!"

I threw on my clothes. I decided not to wake my dad. I would tell him later. I was running to the hospital as fast as I could. What could be wrong? What was he talking about? As I came down the hall toward Joe's room I saw them running beside the gurney — Pete, with my father close behind.

"What is going on? Dad, how long have you been here? All night! What's happening?" I was crying desperately for information but they ran past me. I followed Peter to radiology. The signs read: "CAT Scans/MRI".

I was full of fear. Why was this happening? Pete was finally able to say that Joe had never regained consciousness after the surgery. He thought he saw him have a seizure and heard him grinding his teeth, but his eyes never opened and he did not respond even when the nurses tried to rouse him. He should have woken up by now but he did not.

Oh, God! Oh, God! We were able to watch from behind a glass wall as he went into the MRI tube. When the doctors finally came toward us I could hardly breathe. I had come to recognize this feeling now, the feeling of terror. The doctor told us Joe had a stroke, a complete right hemisphere stroke with partial losses on the left side. There was no activity on the right side of his brain — nothing! This part of his brain died because of either a bleed or an air bubble. He said there would be an investigation to determine why this happened.

For now, he said, "All we can do is wait and see if he wakes." Everyone else was walking down the hall away from me. I stood still in disbelief. What? I am thinking this cannot be! I looked down the hall to see Dad and Pete, the two men in my life that I could count on — my rocks — embracing and falling apart in tears. I thought that if I cried now I would never stop.

Up in the ICU Joe was under constant watch. I was beside myself with grief. I called my friend Patty to tell her, but once I heard her voice all I could do was cry. I could barely get the words out. I remember sitting on the floor of the phone booth sobbing.

It was late when our friends Jeff and Nancy arrived and we all went back to the B&B. The nurses said we had to get some rest and there was nothing we could do at the hospital but sit in the waiting room. They promised to call if they had any news. Even though we brought Dad back to the B&B, we knew that as soon as he could he was going to find his way back to the hospital to sit close by Joe. My father looked worse than I had ever seen him. I had no strength within me to help him. He and Peter seemed to cling to each other in desperation.

Jeff and Nancy stayed with us. We cried and cried until we cried ourselves to sleep. When I awoke, there we were — all four of us — still holding on to one another.

In the morning we went to the hospital and, of course, there was Dad at Joe's bedside. No matter how many times I took him back to the hotel to put him to bed, he always ended up sneaking back to the hospital to sit next to his grandson. The nurses told us, "He prayed in Hebrew and held Joe's hand, never leaving him throughout the night." From that moment we never left Joe's side either, and if one of us had to it was just for a moment. We taped our photos on the sides of his crib so that in case he opened his eyes he would see us. I recorded myself reading his favorite books and singing our favorite songs so that when we left to get something to eat he would still hear our voices, hoping that he could indeed hear us. It was the longest breath I have ever taken, waiting for him to open those eyes — praying , hoping to find my little boy again.

At night we took turns going to the hotel to sleep. One of us was always by Joe's side. We spent eight days watching him breathe, breathe in, breathe out, eyes swollen closed, just laying there. I asked God to take him if he would not wake. What is the purpose of this? You would think that when life throws you this particular wild card, people would surround you with comfort and love, but the nurses and doctors avoided talking to us and averted their eyes. I suppose it was just as hard for them. I needed them more than ever to guide us and they were not able to do that. It was our friends who came and never left our side. My father never once gave up hope and offered his prayers each moment, saying, "It will be all right, I promise you. God will never let me down." I wondered where he found that faith. Where did it come from? Why do I not have that faith? I wanted to believe. I wanted so badly to believe. I still asked God to help us, anyway.

There was no one else who could save us now. We were at the No Hope Hotel, and I was once again living life five minutes at a time. I would look at the clock on the wall. It was 9:00 am. I could hear that clock ticking from the other side of the room. I, of course, was in the *Waiting* room. (I laughed to myself and thought, how aptly named!) At 9:05 I looked at the clock again and realized, as painful as this was, I made it through five more minutes! When the room grew dark, I realized I had made it through another day. I would tell myself that if I can get through just five more minutes, I can get through this day and the next. I felt that things were never changing but, looking closer, I realized that they actually were changing. It just felt like the rest of the world was going about its business and that our world had stopped, everything in my life — our life — was standing still once again.

I did not know then that my faith was emerging. I can see now that this was the beginning. I'm sorry I never had the chance to ask my father about his faith. I took it for granted that he always had it, that he was born with it; but now I know something must have happened to him for him to have found it. I do not think true faith is something you are given, but must be something you search for and find on your own.

As always he sat by Joe's crib during the night, even when he promised me he would stay in the hotel and get some sleep. The nurses eventually told me that he was there every night. Holding onto Joe's finger, he prayed through the night. He would say he had magic words for God, *macachouri machacha,* over and over. He said, "You must believe and ask God to help you. He is listening for your prayers." I wished I could believe; I just didn't know how.

"Why? Tell me why, Dad, if there is a God, why does he send a baby with a broken heart? Why would he hurt this innocent baby? What could I, Pete or Joe have done to possibly deserve this? How much can one suffer and where does it begin? And where does it end? Tell me, Dad! I want to believe in something. I would believe if you could just help me understand these things. Take this pain away!"

He never did give me an answer. At least, not in a way that satisfied me. He shrugged his shoulders and said, "HE has a reason, I am sure. We just don't know it yet."

I wanted so badly for him to have an answer for me, an answer that would make some sense.

I began to realize that when I was asking God for help it was really an empty thought, meaningless words to me — something I was in the habit of saying when things went wrong. I did not ask God for help really thinking there would be a response and an answer to my prayer. It wasn't even a meaningful prayer, just something to say, I guess. Like when you are walking down the hallway in the hospital and someone passes by you quickly and asks, "How are you doing?" They don't expect an answer because they don't slow down. They are walking away as you're blankly answering, "Fine, thank you," but really wishing you could say the truth and be heard: "My fucking world just fell apart and you're smugly asking how I am when you don't really

[90]

want to know!" It's something we do unconsciously; something we all do.

Sitting in the waiting room, I remembered my mother's words when she invited me to her party. "While the music's playing, dance!" The music *is* still playing, I said to myself over and over. Joe didn't die, so I still have some music, right? I would ask myself, "What is in my control today?" Not a whole lot I thought! Sometimes it was what food I chose to eat, the magazine I read, sometimes just the tiniest pleasure — pleasures I used to take for granted. As long as I thought of something that I controlled, that I *could* control, I was okay.

It had been eight days. The doctor said Joe's brain was swollen. The swelling had to go down. Once it did they would have a better idea of his prognosis. The good news, they said, is that his heart is stable. It was hard to swallow anything as "good news!"

I was walking down the hall one day when I saw the cutest little dog. Immediately I was drawn to it; I missed my dogs so much. But this dog, in such an unlikely place, attracted me — distracted me — from my current reality. "Can I pet your dog? What's its name?"

"Her name is Snickers," the owner said.

"What are you doing here"? I asked.

"Snickers is visiting. She is part of a pet therapy program. My name is Pat," the woman said with a great smile.

I played with Snickers for about ten minutes.

"Oh, I love dogs. I miss mine so much," I told her. "Well, what are you doing here? Do you live around here?" she asked.

"No," I said, realizing that for those few moments playing with Snickers on the floor of the hospital hallway I had forgotten all my troubles. Her question woke me to my reality. I told her a little about Joe being in the ICU, that he had suffered a stroke and was in a coma. Then a light went on in my head. I am sure that she could see me thinking!

I said, "Hey, Pat, can you and Snickers come in the ICU and meet Joe?"

"Well, we have never been in there before, but I don't see why not. Let me ask!"

The next thing I knew we were walking through those double electronic doors towards Joe's bed with the cutest little terrier.

Pat held Snickers up as I said, "Joe, you won't believe what I just found in the hospital. It's the cutest little dog I have ever seen! Her name is Snickers. If you open your eyes you can see her. Momma is going to move your hand to her back so you can feel how soft she is." As I moved his little hand onto Snickers' back for him to feel her I said, "Joe, have you ever heard of anything so silly? A dog in the hospital, in your bed!"

The moment I said it — maybe it was the moment his hand touched Snickers' fur — we all heard Joe giggle! A nurse was standing there and she heard it too! Otherwise I don't think anyone would have believed it really happened.

[92]

Then, between tears, I said, "Joe, when you open your eyes you will see how cute she is." I had hoped at that moment his eyes would open, but they didn't.

Everyone was so happy to hear that little giggle that Pat said she and Snickers would be back every day to visit Joe for as long as he was in the hospital.

I tried to take a walk outside the hospital at least once each day. I craved to see something — anything! — outside the hospital. To smell and feel the fresh air or to watch people coming and going, just doing normal things, gave me a sense that life was continuing somewhere. When we spoke to Kate she would always ask to speak to Joe. We would tell her he was sleeping and that we would call her when he woke up. Pete's mother would then tell her that we had called when she was out playing or at school. I thought it was going to be horrible for all of us if Joe did not wake up soon. How would we ever explain this to her?

One morning, while walking outside, I noticed a car with a Colorado license plate. The car had a bumper sticker that said: EXPECT A MIRACLE. Okay, I thought, I will — I will expect a miracle! Once back in the hospital and upstairs I had already forgotten about that car and its bumper sticker. Pete and I asked the nurse if we could give Joe a bath. It had been so many days that he had gone without a bath and he loved bath time! I think we were desperately trying to find something that we could do for Joe ourselves.

"Of course," she said. "There's a tub around the corner."

[93]

We ran the water all the while telling Joe, "That is the water running for your bath. I bet this will feel so good, Joe!" We put very little water in the tub because he still had to be lying down. I thought he would love the feeling of the warm water and being washed and clean. The nurse was supporting his head under her arm and I was bathing him. When I turned my head and looked at Joe I could see that he was peeking at me through his eyelids. His eyes were still closed but I saw him peeking.

"LOOK, everyone! Joe is opening his eyes for us. Today he's going to open his eyes. Wow, Joe, you will get to see how cute Snickers is when she comes for a visit today."

It was slow going, but he did open his eyes. Once his eyes were open the nurse had an idea to see if he could bear any weight on his legs if we tried to stand him on his feet. He was so weak but we were sure that he was trying. Each day we seemed to move an inch farther. For us, each inch represented a mile!

Snickers came every day to visit and they became fast and great friends. So, too, had Snickers' owner, Pat, and I.

Pat told me, "Deena, this experience has changed me — changed my life in more ways than you will ever know!"

Joe had a nasogastric feeding tube in his nose to deliver nutrition in the form of liquid food. I had asked the nurses to pull the tube so that I could feed him. They refused.

"Mrs. Hoagland, that is against doctor's orders. We cannot do that!"

Frustrated and angry, I would answer, "If you keep giving him that stuff he will never feel hunger and if he is not hungry why would he learn to swallow again?"

We argued back and forth. I felt I had no choice. They were not listening and, yes, I was being difficult; but I was sure that Joe would eat if that tube was not there. So I told them once and for all, "Okay, if you're not going to take it out, I WILL!"

"I'll have to call the doctor," the nurse said.

"Look, I promise I'm not going to let him starve. If I cannot get him to swallow, you can put it back. But *please* let me try!"

Finally, they agreed. Pete went down to the cafeteria and got Joe chocolate frozen yogurt.

I told Joe, "Buddy, I bet you are so hungry, you are going to *love* this. Ice cream. You can even share some with Snickers."

Joe loved every bit of it. Liquids were hard for him to swallow — he would choke on them — so we stuck to pudding and ice cream and yogurt. The feeding tube never went back in.

When the doctors began talking about discharging Joe, he was able to sit upright when propped with pillows. The left side of his body was completely paralyzed. The right side of his body had weakened. He was able to talk even though the left side of his face drooped. At discharge, the doctors wanted Joe to go directly to a rehabilitation hospital in Florida. Our problem was that the rehab hospital was two hours from where we lived. We told the doctors there was no way we could do that. Kate was seven years old and needed us too, and Pete had to work and we wouldn't leave Joe by himself! It was unrealistic!

Joe's neurologist gave us a three-page report filled with "Nevers": Joe will never sing. Joe will never see the food on the left side of his plate. Joe will probably never walk, and if he does he will limp. Joe will never run. Joe will never play sports. He will ignore the left side of his papers, books, tests and schoolwork. There was not much encouragement in that report. Finally, after much disagreement and discussion, and against medical advisement, the doctors agreed to discharge Joe into our care.

This time, our homecoming didn't feel completely triumphant. We still had so many things to figure out. We were worried about telling Kate and our friends about Joe. The hospital was worried we might sue them. Pete and I thought about it — sure we did. Though, in the end, neither of us had the energy to think about fighting anyone. Besides, the doctor had tried to do his best. How could we place blame? We knew it was going to be difficult helping Joe find his way back to himself. We also knew that if there were only five surgeons in the country who could help him, and if we were truly with the best, then making enemies was not a good idea. We were going to need all these people on our team.

Joe was happy to be home. He was excited to see Kate, our dogs and our friends. When Kate asked what happened to him, Joe answered simply, in a matter-of-fact way, "I broke."

[96]

Therapists came in and out. They all said the same thing: "He is resistant . . . noncompliant . . . difficult to work with . . . he refuses . . ."

Whenever I asked Joe, "Why won't you do what they ask you to do?" he would answer defiantly, "They're stupid! All they do is ask me to do things they know I can't do, Mom!"

Pete went back to work at the fish farm. We were about to move to our new place in the Keys, with no friends and nothing familiar, with an anxious seven-year-old, and a three-year-old with a heart problem who was paralyzed and visually impaired. I was less than excited, to say the least.

Kate grew distant. She had never been this way ever before. No matter how hard I tried to engage her, she kept to herself. I guessed she needed time to process everything. I knew I needed time also, so I tried not to push her. But I missed our snuggling and closeness. I could see she was struggling, but I couldn't force it out of her; it would have to come in its own time. In between packing for our move to Key Largo and Joe's therapy appointments that were going terribly, I would prop Joe in bed and let him watch his favorite cartoons. It was the only way I could get anything done.

I don't know what it was that set her off. I am not sure that it was anything at all specifically or if it was just her time to blow, but one day Kate came into the kitchen, stood her ground in front of me and announced as angrily as she could muster, "I HATE YOU, I HATE YOU, I HATE YOU!"

[97]

"Kate, what's this about? What's wrong?"(As if I didn't know!)

And then it came pouring out, uncontrollably, like a flood from a broken dam. It seemed like it would never stop. "You broke him. You said they were fixing him, but you broke him!"

All I could do was hold her in my arms. We sat on the kitchen floor, rocking back and forth. We both cried and cried and when it was possible I whispered between tears, "They tried to fix his heart, Kate. They did not mean to hurt him. Nobody meant to hurt him. It was an accident. We are all going to do our best to help him, I promise."

Me, in college, when I first met Pete

Me and Pete, Colorado,1974

My
father:
Manny
Rosen

Four Generations:
My mother Miriam, me, Grandma Annie and Kate

Me (pregnant with Joe) and Pete
on our 10th wedding anniversary

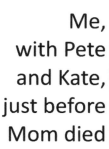Me,
with Pete
and Kate,
just before
Mom died

In the hospital, with newborn Joe

After Joe's first surgery

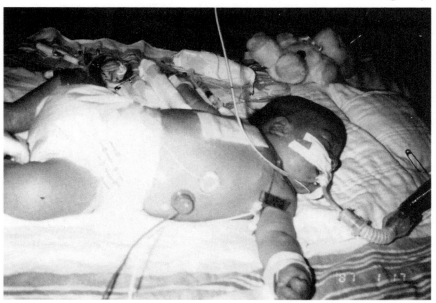

One of Pete's
visits home;
before Joe's
second surgery

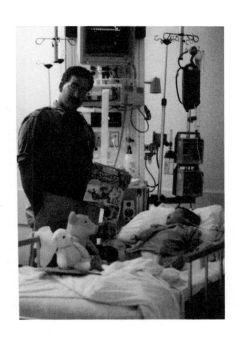

Another
hospitalization,
another surgery

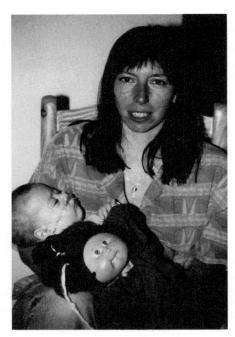

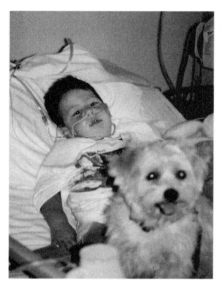

Joe,
with his
hospital pal
Snickers

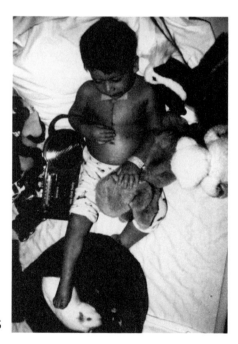

Distracted
by toys

Kate and Joe, discovering some joy at the holidays

One Breath Away

We are always just one breath away. From one breath to the next, one moment to the next, life can change. Why do we not know how important each moment is? We never know until we have to know. Then, whenever something huge happens in our lives — the important moments — we remember them as if in slow motion; aware of the smells, the sounds, that moment itself when life stopped, when life changed.

So many moments in life are taken for granted. The next breath we take can bring love, disaster or something beautiful. If only I knew to celebrate each breath as if it were the first, or possibly the last, how much greater life would be! How many breaths have I wasted wanting something I did not have, dreaming of what-if, or living in fear. If only I could celebrate this breath I would realize — have realized! — so much sooner that this breath is the only one that counts right now; the only one I have right now. How much easier and more meaningful would this life have become? We are all just one breath away from something meaningful, something big, all of the time. Hadn't that already happened to me?

In one breath, life changed. I am beginning to remember those breaths that have counted in my life:

Birth . . . Death . . . Sighs . . . Deep breaths . . . Coming up for air

Although the world is full of suffering,
it is full also of the overcoming of it.

~Helen Keller

Part Two: *Fonzie, Sea-beans and Dolphin Dreams*

Palm trees and coconuts, desperation and nevers

I look back at that time and wonder how Pete and I lived through it. We laughed whenever we could. We loved a lot — more than most people, I think. While many of our friends divorced — and are divorcing, right and left — we clung to each other knowing that on some days all we had was each other. For that I am filled with gratitude, ever aware of my good fortune.

We arrived in Key Largo in 1990, when the community was still considered rural. Just one hour south of Miami, it seemed like another country somewhere in the Caribbean, not a part of Florida at all. Pete was working at the fish farm, sometimes as much as 72 hours a week! I was unpacking boxes in a foreign town. Kate started second grade. We knew not a single soul in our new town; starting out with no friends and a broken child. I suppose all my family had broken hearts and were feeling immobilized. It was a sad time with Joe paralyzed and visually impaired, needing total care. He often wept for no apparent reason. He had to be propped up and carried everywhere. He was an infant again.

The doctors had given us their report to share with therapists and the school, the three pages of "Nevers": If he walks he will walk with a limp, but he will never run. He will never sing. He will never show emotion. He will never look at the left side of his school papers so he will likely fail often. He will never dance. He will never look to his left when crossing a street. He will never be able to solve problems logically. He will NEVER and NEVER and NEVER!

I was not sure what to do. What *was* certain was that I felt desperate and alone. I had to force myself to believe that things would get better. It was difficult to face each day otherwise. But, I got mad and I got depressed. I only allowed myself to cry in the shower. Water beat down on my body as I crouched in the corner and sobbed until there was no more hot water and no more tears to cry. Then I'd dry my eyes, get dressed and move on.

But desperation pushes us all beyond our limits, past what we know. Wanting so much more for all of us, I found myself with no choice but to be "creative" with Joe's condition.

◊   ◊   ◊

Help is on the way

He was curious. He was lonely too. His family — his pod — had been gone a long time now. He had fallen behind trying to keep up but couldn't. He was used to the sound of the motors but the men on board sounded different. They were excited, hurried. What were they talking about? As he swam closer to get a better look, the boat whirled in circles around him and then stopped. What was happening? The men were talking again and he decided to swim even closer.

[112]

He remained still when they entered the water, approaching him slowly. Then he saw the fish they held in their hands. He was hungry and so tired. He swam right up to them and ate all the fish they could fed him. As the men would later tell the story, "He swam right into our arms."

Soon they brought him to a new lagoon where there were other dolphins, although none that he recognized. One by one they greeted him. He no longer felt alone and isolated! There was much chatter among them. In the days to come many people arrived who stood above and looked at him. Some even tried to swim with him. He got closer to them each time. Soon he began to play with the people who came to swim in the lagoon and to play with the other dolphins as well. They bonded to form a new kind of pod, a new family.

Plunge

Joe had always loved to swim. He loved water and animals more than anything. I thought the water and swimming might help him move his body and develop muscle tone. In some places he was floppy. The left side of his face drooped. His legs were floppy, but his left hand was closed tight and his left arm was bent and locked at the elbow, making them useless. At the very least, maybe he could have a little fun. Clearly there wasn't much fun for any of us these days, but especially for Joe.

I had been taking him to hotel pools in Key Largo until we were asked to leave by the managers.

"I'm sorry, ma'am. It's depressing for our guests."

I understood, but I was mad. Then I heard about a place called Dolphins Plus, where people swim with dolphins in a natural lagoon. I called them and spoke with the owner, Lloyd, a gruff sounding man. He said to come down and talk to him someday. I don't know why, but when I hung up the phone, "someday" became TODAY for me. I drove Joe there in the next few minutes. I had no idea what was there or what would happen, but I was clearly a mom on a mission.

When I arrived, Lloyd took one look at Joe and said, "I said 'some day.' I didn't mean today!"

I wanted to tell him, I wanted to shout: BUT I DON'T HAVE SOME DAY!" Those words ("someday" = "future") no longer had meaning in my dictionary.

Joe slumped in my arms; my eyes welled with tears. I must have looked pathetic and desperate, and he realized I was about to fall apart. "Okay, okay" he sighed. "Come on in," he relented, with obvious reluctance. I didn't know what to expect. In fact, I'd never been close to a dolphin before.

The front office was a small room. There was a *chicki* hut and an enclosed thing that looked like a phone booth. Later I learned this was where Lloyd would stand as he checked in the people who came to swim with the dolphins. There were swim fins, masks and snorkels hanging on the wall and rows of picnic benches. It was really a funky place. Then I saw the lagoon where the dolphins lived.

Lloyd was a small man with a weathered, deep-lined face and curly gray hair. He seemed so gruff and irritable. He introduced me to his wife. "Call me Oma," she said. "Everyone calls me Oma!" How sweet, I thought. *Oma* is the German word for grandma.

"She's my 'Squirt'," Lloyd said, winking at her. This was the first indication that maybe he was really a nice guy hiding behind that salty toughness. Oma proceeded to tell me that one of the dolphins is named "Squirt," after her. "There they are," she tells me, pointing toward the lagoon. "I can whistle and Fonzie and Squirt will swim right to me!" But, she added, she never swims with them.

Just then, Lloyd showed up again from around the corner, carrying a large bucket of fish. Then he brought us down to the dock to meet the dolphins.

In the heat of that day, with all the turmoil surrounding me and my family, suddenly there existed only a bucket of fish, a man named Lloyd, Joe and me. That moment, when Joe met Fonzie, our lives changed.

Fonzie came up to the edge of the platform, enormous, yet graceful, to meet Joe. He appeared to push the other dolphins away from the dock and away from Joe. Most three-year-olds might be intimidated, but Joe giggled — the first sign of a smile in months. He wanted to give Fonzie a fish. He wanted to touch him, to be with him. It was a moment that stopped time. Life began again as we heard ourselves laughing.

Lloyd encouraged us to touch Fonzie. While holding Joe in my lap with one arm, I extended my free hand toward the dolphin. He swam close and gently brushed against my palm, allowing me to touch the full length of his body. I was amazed and surprised that he didn't feel the way I expected at all. I thought he would feel like a fish but, no, it was more like the texture of a freshly peeled hard-boiled egg! So strong and purposeful a being, and yet so sensitive, he seemed to be reaching out to us as well. I was wondering if he wanted this contact with us as much as we wanted it with him. I was lost in the moment.

I did not realize it then, but at that very moment I was learning how important laughter and joy are. I did not know then that one day I would teach others that recovery is not just about medicine or being cured; but also about the ability to have joy no matter what the circumstances, no matter how out-of-control our lives are. I did not know then that a dolphin and a three-year-old boy would be my teachers. But I was the student and class had just begun. There were many metaphors unfolding before me. I was feeling so many things all at once. I could hear me telling myself to pay attention.

I remember looking at Fonzie, thinking about his beauty and enormity, and I thought, too, about what we seemed to have in common. Hadn't we both been taken from the lives we thought we had, the lives we thought we were going to have? I assumed this must be true for Fonzie. But, unlike Fonzie, who seemed so joyful and playful, I wasn't coping well in my new life. I was feeling trapped and confined — held hostage in this new life and feeling out of control. I had begun to wonder if perhaps there was no such thing as control after all.

Joe, too, was trapped, restrained within a body that would not function. Would this define our family now? What did it all mean? Fonzie seemed so content. How did he do it? How did he feel? I wanted to know.

In Fonzie, Joe found a friend. They were instant pals. Fonzie appeared to love Joe's giggle and the little meatball body with fragile legs and arms that didn't work like the others. He accepted Joe just the way he was. For Joe that was a gift — unconditional love.

As much as I tried not to show disappointment, I so longed for Joe to be well again. And Joe knew this. No matter how hard he tried to do something, to *be* some way, he knew that he was, in a big way, the cause for my sadness. And Fonzie had also found a friend who loved him completely and without reservation. It was later that I thought Fonzie was very misunderstood. He was a teenager, a character, aloof in the way human teens can be. For some reason he was not the most popular of the dolphins; not only with the dolphin handlers but with the other dolphins as well. He was the low man on the totem pole. But with Joe in his life, Fonzie's best side began to show.

Theirs was a pivotal meeting and relationship. Interestingly enough, this meeting gave us all another chance, an opportunity to see things — even the pain and sadness — differently, and to be seen differently. At the time I had no idea that there was opportunity emerging out of the darkness.

When it was time to leave an hour later, Lloyd looked at me. My eyes were again full of tears.

"*Now* why are you crying?" he asked. "I don't like it when women cry!"

He was so rough around the edges. I had never met anyone like him before. I told him what I had seen happen between Joe and Fonzie.

"This is the first time I have heard Joe's sweet little giggle since he had the stroke."

Lloyd looked at me and in such a matter-of-fact way asked, "So when can you come back?"

Those words took my breath away.

Joe and I went as often as possible to visit with Fonzie. Clearly inspired by this beautiful dolphin, Joe began to work hard at his recovery. He wanted to be able to play with Fonzie and to feed him. We worked hard together so that Joe could learn to sit on his own without the support of pillows or someone to lean against. We practiced sitting every day.

I began finding new ways of having fun with Joe. We found a new beginning as mother and son. We played as many games as we could think of on the dock. I told Joe that Fonzie was a left-handed dolphin. I told Joe that if he wanted to play with Fonzie he would have to use his left hand or Fonzie would not be able to play! Joe thought this was funny, but he believed me because I am his mother and also because he was just three years old. Together we came up with a lot of left-handed games to play with Fonzie.

I watched in awe as an incredible friendship between this magnificent dolphin and a fragile little boy unfolded.

With each achievement I would think this might be all we could get, but let's just keep trying. After all, we were already crossing things off that list of "Nevers". There were so many ups and downs; little signs that we were making progress but then sometimes Joe would lose the skill and regress. At times it seemed that just a change in the weather — a cold front or storm might be enough to set him back. On those days Joe would become frustrated and cry.

I would tell him, "Everyone has bad days, Joe. You will see that if you did it before you can do it again!"

I, too, needed the encouragement so that I would not forget. Most of our days were now filled to the brim with hope.

Joe so wanted to swim with Fonzie.

"Well, Kiddo, I guess you are going to have to learn to walk and use those legs!"

He would smile and say, "Fonzie is going to be so surprised when he sees what I can do!"

As soon as he was able to sit on his own without falling over, we began trying to get him to bear weight on his legs and stand. He was slowly gaining upper body strength. Our biggest triumph was when he *did* begin to stand! Then we had hope that one day he might take a few steps without falling — maybe even learn to walk again!

In the beginning we helped him by allowing him to lean on us. This provided him with the support he needed, not just physically, but mentally as well. He began to believe he could do it. It was hard for him to balance, especially when the dolphins jumped and played causing the floating dock to move from side to side and up and down.

Whenever he lost his balance and fell, which was often, he would laugh his head off! I would tell Joe that Fonzie was just trying to get him to fall in the water so they could swim together! This was great therapy for Joe. Eventually he could sit and stand on his own without toppling over — another miracle!

While holding his hands and walking behind him, I would say, "Joe, you take two steps and then mama will carry you for two steps more."

And that is how we went everywhere! It was devastating to watch. It always took triple the amount of time to get anywhere, but we seemed to have a lot of time back then.

One day, Debby, an old friend from Denver, came to visit. We sat in the yard and talked while Joe sat on my lap. Eventually Joe wanted to go back into the house to watch cartoons, he was so tired. Debby watched as we walked two steps at a time.

Sometimes he said, "I can do it myself!"

"Okay, show me!"

He tried so hard and then he fell.

When Joe was sleeping Debby said, "Maybe you are being too hard on him. Maybe he is not going to walk! Do you ever wonder if you are pushing him too hard?"

She had watched him lose his balance and fall several times and it broke her heart to see it.

"Sure, of course I do. But how will I know if he can or will if we don't try!"

We *had* to try. We tried every day. And every day I would say, "We love you just the way you are, Joe! It's okay if you don't learn to walk. We will all love you just the way you are! But let's just try."

He would look up at me and say, "Okay, Mama, I love you too!"

Little by little it appeared that Joe was gaining more strength. When he could take two steps, we graduated to three and then to four.

Joe and I collected sea-beans for Fonzie whenever we were near the shore. Sea-beans are seeds, officially known as *propagules*, from the mangrove tree. They drop from the trees and collect near the shoreline. Dolphins don't eat them, but Fonzie loved playing with them, the way a dog likes to fetch a ball. We collected bags and bags of them. Finding sea-beans was a great opportunity for Joe to try to look all around left and right! When he found one on the left I would bend down and pick it up. He was becoming stronger and beginning to try to bend on his own.

He would announce, "Fonzie will love these beans! I can't wait for him to see what I can do now!"

We worked hard on getting his left arm to come down by his side. It did not seem to be working. I would tell Joe we could take turns with "righty then lefty." I would have to help Joe by placing things in his left hand and on his arm at first. Each day we tried and tried. We would work on reaching for things with his left arm. I would purposely put things just out of his reach on his left side so he would look for them and try to get them himself. I began to see a little movement.

Eventually I saw Joe use his right hand to pull his left arm down! Then with his right hand he would place objects on his left arm. We tried opening his left hand to hold things. It was difficult to watch. Not because it was painful, but because he was trying so hard to succeed and it seemed like it was never going to happen. At night I would hear Joe talking to himself before falling asleep.

He would say over and over, "Just keep trying. You can do it."

Whenever they heard someone use the word "never," Kate and Joe would announce, "'Never' is not a word we use in our house!"

Joe was the "I-Can-Do Kid" and we were all so proud of him. Kate would add, emphatically, "And we're The Hoaglands!"

When finally we were invited to go into the water and swim with the dolphins, I was certain Fonzie was somehow communicating to the other dolphins that Joe was *his* friend; that it was *their* play date and the others should stay away. Fonzie would poke at Joe's left leg. Then he would swim to Joe's right side and poke that leg too. He would push on Joe's butt! Joe giggled the entire time. I whispered to Fonzie, thanking him for being Joe's best friend. I told him if ever he needed me I would be there for him.

Everything Joe achieved involved Fonzie in one way or another.

Sea-beans were Fonzie's favorite toys. I would put a sea-bean in Joe's left hand. While swimming with Joe in my arms, Fonzie would sneak up next to Joe and pull the sea-bean out of Joe's left hand while it was still shut tight. Joe would laugh his head off! Once home from our swimming adventure Joe would talk about Fonzie for the rest of the day!

He would ask me, "Mama, what is Fonzie doing now?"

At night he would ask me if I thought Fonzie was afraid of the dark. Even I could not stop talking about Fonzie and the other dolphins. Pete would come home from work and Kate from school to Joe and me telling Fonzie stories. Pete was a little doubtful at first, but once he saw Joe's progress he became really interested. Kate was also excited and couldn't wait for a day off from school when we could all go together. They soon joined Joe and me in the water with the dolphins. It was extraordinary watching all of us laugh again!

[123]

Whenever we got in the water with Fonzie and the dolphins, Joe and I would pretend we were dolphins. Joe would hold onto my neck as best he could and we would dive down together! Joe always came up laughing! The first thing Fonzie would do is push on Joe's legs which made Joe want to swim with him even more. By now Fonzie's trainers were offering to have Joe come play with Fonzie during their lunch hours. Watching Joe and Fonzie's relationship was extraordinary for everyone involved.

Months later, one of the trainers had the idea to have Joe carry Fonzie a bucket of fish! She put a small fish in the smallest bucket she could find. We helped Joe hang it on his left arm and had him carry it to his friend, the Fonz. Joe was so excited! Each day the trainers would add more fish to the bucket making it heavier and more challenging for him. Eventually Joe was able to bring his arm down by his side! Joe's left hand was the hardest to work with and the slowest to come back. It took years of hard work.

We told Joe, "If you want to feed Fonzie, you have to do it with your left hand." At first we had to pry open his hand to put a fish in it, and then assist him to reach out over the dock so that Fonzie could grab it. Just like all of our Fonzie games, this took a long time before we saw any progress. It was slow going but they never seemed to tire of the left-handed games or the swims they enjoyed together as the reward for their hard work.

It was soon time for another check-up with Joe's neurologist. Joe would become anxious on long car rides;

after all, the only times that he could remember being in the car that long was whenever we went to the hospital. Once we were in the doctors' office I watched the doctor looking over Joe's chart. He was flipping the pages, eyeing Joe, then flipping pages again. Then he asked Joe if he wanted to sit on the floor and play with him a little.

After a few minutes he looked up at me and said, "Mrs. Hoagland, this is just *amazing*! Joe has made unbelievable progress! Who is his therapist? I must speak with him. I want to know every technique he is using with Joe. I am dumfounded. This is just amazing!"

I was clearly nervous to tell him the truth. What would he think? How could I explain it all, and in just a few minutes? But I told him about meeting Fonzie and all the things we had been doing. He was fascinated and said he wanted to come and see for himself.

When we left the hospital that day we had a little skip in our hearts and felt lighter. Joe was hungry and said he wanted to eat steak! So steak it was! I cut the steak and put it on the left side of his plate; vegetables were on the right. Joe ate every bit of steak! Cross that off the list too!

On the way home Joe asked us, "Is it 'your ami'? Or is it 'my ami'?" Pete and I laughed and laughed. Joe was not so sure what we were laughing about but he laughed too. When we composed ourselves we explained that Miami is the name of the city! We weren't sure he understood that for a long time.

Our focus had changed: we were no longer anguishing over Joe's recovery, but relishing these incredible moments together. Fonzie and his friends were a vitamin of courage and a dose of joy. The dolphins embraced us, and each day we were getting closer to becoming whole again.

Dolphin dreams come true

I was now back in a small private practice and working again while the kids were at school. Pete was still working at the fish farm. Kate was making friends in school and Joe was in preschool steadily finding his way. With persistence we could see him recovering the use of his left side more and more.

During this time my father began dating! He had a special lady friend named Pearl. I was happy to see him moving on and finding companionship. At nearly 87 years old I was not sure he had really found true love with a woman in Palm Beach 30 years younger, but who was I to judge? He had accepted Pete and so I told myself I should celebrate the fact that he was happy and not alone

Lloyd and I thought that one day we might create a not-for-profit organization to help others like Joe. Lloyd thought it was a good idea. Not only would we be helping others, but we would then have a way to pay for the dolphin time we were using.

Whenever my clients didn't have insurance or the money to pay for therapy I suggested they put what they could afford in the dolphin cookie jar in my waiting room. I explained that this money would pay to bring children and their families who needed therapy to swim with the dolphins. Whenever I didn't have enough money to pay for all the swims, Lloyd didn't seemed to mind. He was grateful that I was trying. Each week we brought children who lived in the children's shelter, a place provided by the county for emergency placement of children removed from their homes due to abuse or neglect until proper foster families could be found. We started a "Mommy & Me" group dolphin swim for children in Joe's preschool class which was a class for children with special needs. People who heard about what we were doing often came to watch. Lloyd was proud to tell others of the program and of the progress the children were making. People would leave Dolphins Plus, tell someone what they had seen and then even more people would show up to watch.

Requests for swims for others with special needs, like Joe, started coming in. I was thrilled to be helping others and felt it was my way to give back.

One day a woman who had been watching asked if she could interview me for an article. "Of course," I said. This would be a wonderful way for Dolphins Plus to get some publicity and maybe someone who reads the article would send us money to continue our work. This work was so rewarding to me and to others, I was rapidly realizing this was a new form of therapy that could help many people like us. The article appeared on a Sunday morning in newspapers around the country! By the following Wednesday we had received over 2,000 letters from readers mostly asking for help for their child, or for someone they knew. There were many phone calls too. I continued to volunteer and help whenever someone came to the facility. Lloyd would call me to help someone in the water.

There were many discussions about whether or not we should begin a business or not-for-profit organization so that we could afford to keep it all going. Each time the subject came up, I declined. And for so many reasons.

I was struggling.

I didn't know what to do or how to begin. I was so overwhelmed with caring for Joe and my family, how could I possibly take on anything else? I had huge medical bills to pay and I had to work. I would never be able to fit it all in. I could barely get through my daily list of things to do as it was. But my mind kept going back to the idea of starting a therapy program. Each time I thought about it I kept thinking that if we really do this, it would have to become a not-for-profit organization in order to help other families like ours. It was the only way I could feel comfortable because it just didn't seem right to charge for this kind of therapy. It had been given to us, so I felt it should be a gift to others. I knew all about the stress of large medical and therapy bills. Those bills don't go away; they just keep mounting. I thought that if we were to form a not-for-profit, then maybe I would be able to raise money by writing grants and getting donations to offset the cost of therapy for the families. But there would be other costs, also. How could I possibly raise all the money that would be needed to properly care for the dolphins? Just those thoughts alone were overwhelming.

Yet, I couldn't stop thinking about it.

My mind was reeling with ideas. Joe and I had worked very hard at so many things throughout each and every day. In the beginning, he was only motivated to make every activity about Fonzie and his friends. I thought about adding a formal therapy component to supplement each swim. I began to write down all the ideas we had already come up with. I knew that one swim would never be enough. In order to truly help someone, and for it to be therapeutic, there has to be more than one session, yet still remain fun enough to be motivating. But what if I put this all together and other people didn't get better? It would be wrong to promise anyone anything. Families like mine search for any answer or a shred of hope to hang onto. There's a fine balance. How could I communicate what this had done for us, yet still help others to be realistic about what it could do for them? We all need hope and joy — the two things I hadn't realized had been lost in our own lives.

Where would Joe be if Pete and I believed that awful list the doctors gave us? What if we had not tried? What would have happened if I had not stumbled into Fonzie's world? Deep down I knew this was my calling.

Unconsciously I was already developing a curriculum and therapy program. I just hadn't acknowledged it to myself yet. I kept telling myself that I had to be realistic. Most of all, I didn't want to start something and not be able to finish it. I was afraid of failing. Disappointing Lloyd or the children and their families would crush me. What if Joe needed more surgery while I was in the middle of putting it all together? What if he had another stroke and I had to drop it. It's not like these things hadn't already happened. I had to drop everything once before, make a run for Joes' life and leave everything behind. It was unexpected, and for good reason, but even so it hurt my clients and it hurt me. I did not want to set myself up for the kind of added stress. The timing just wasn't right and I didn't think it would *ever* be right. We were still recovering from Joe's last surgery — physically, emotionally and financially. I knew there was another surgery coming, but I didn't know when. It was always looming over us and I could feel my anxiety build before every visit to the cardiologist for Joe's regular check-ups.

Only when we left the hospital with good news could I feel myself begin to breathe again. Three weeks before each appointment I was sleepless with a feeling of dread. I noticed the appointments were getting closer to one another and realized that the doctors were already making plans without saying much to us. I remembered them telling us early on that he would have to have three surgeries in his life. But he has had three already! I remember thinking that things don't always go the way they are planned or the way they say they will. I found myself living from one doctor's appointment to the next, instead of focusing on the in-between moments.

It was at our next doctor's appointment that they scheduled his impending surgery to replace his aortic valve with a mechanical St. Jude valve. This time I couldn't shake the tears away as easily. I woke up crying, I cried in the shower. I choked back tears, whether dropping the kids off at school or watching TV commercials. Still, nobody knew. I cried only when I was alone. I cried softly. I cried so much.

One afternoon while sitting in the yard, staring out at the calm water, I was unaware of much around me. I heard the messages in my head, over and over, the fear of Joe dying, not making it through this time. I wondered how many times they could do this to him. How much can one's heart take? . . . his *and* ours?

Then I heard him singing.

I looked around as if I had been gone for some time, and there he was — Joe, on the swings singing and swinging and having a great time!

Then I heard the voice in my head that speaks so loudly, "Well, you can sit here and cry all you want. You can worry all you want to. You can't predict the future and you can't change the past. What you have right now is *this* moment. *Your child is singing!*"

I suddenly remembered my mother, her music still playing. I dried my eyes, got up and sang with him.

When I told Lloyd about Joe's surgery, I could see he was moved and holding back emotion. I remember him telling me how he hates it when people cry, so I don't. Joe and I decide it's important to tell Fonzie that he will be away for a little while.

Joe was anxious to see Fonzie and ran to the dock with the trainers. We could hear him talking to Fonzie as he was feeding him, taking turns with righty and lefty.

"I'm gonna be gone for awhile, Fonz. But I'll be back as soon as I can! This time I'm getting a fixed heart and I'm not gonna be broken anymore!"

Lloyd gave us a videotape of Fonzie swimming under water that he had made for Joe. "Joe will love this once he is up and around," he said. "This way he won't have to miss Fonzie so much!"

We joked about whether or not we should have made a video of Joe for Fonzie!

After Joe's surgery Pete and I were allowed to go into intensive care for a short visit. I could see that he was resting and his eyes were closed. He was sleeping. Even though the nurses assure me that he was doing fine I remember all too well how we sat by his bed waiting for his eyes to open after the last surgery, and they didn't. No matter what the nurses said, I would remain anxious until his eyes opened and I could hear him speak. They assured us that everything was fine and that the surgery went well. Making small talk we told them about Joe and Fonzie and I gave them the video Lloyd made.

"If Peter and I are not here when he wakes up, maybe you can play the video for Joe until we arrive?"

The staff was excited to see the video so they popped it in the machine right away. Everyone in the ICU crowded around to see Joe's friend Fonzie!

"Check this out! Joe's vitals are all normal now!"

The resident had noticed that Joe's vital signs had changed as soon as the video began!

[132]

Once we arrived back in Key Largo the first thing Joe wanted to do was tell Fonzie he was home.

My first swim

It was just a few weeks after Joe and I began our adventures with Fonzie that one of the trainers asked, "Why don't you go in the water today?"

"Really? Just me?"

"Sure. Maybe Fonzie and his friends would like to meet you as Deena — *just* Deena – and not Joe's mom."

Huh, I thought. Okay, sure. Why not? I slid into the water, masked and finned. In an instant they are there; enormous, sleek, swiftly brushing against my side, beckoning me to stay with them, dive with them, look into their soulful eyes. I discover that I'm unable to multi-task — I cannot think of anything else. They are the moment. Right now! All I can do is think about staying above water, under water, breathing, and feeling their touch. Where are they now? It's all happening in the moment, and this is the *only* moment, carrying me away (better than sleep)! I am conscious. I am happy for this moment. I have no worries, no future and no past. There's only *now*. This moment is beautiful, happily immersed in the splendid real and raw. And I feel close to something BIG — something in my mind — about why I am here!

Drying off alone, I am thinking again: For those thirty minutes I was free! I don't remember worrying about anything for even one second. I search for God again as if, like loose change, God can be found in the bottom of my purse! He's there somewhere, right? I ache to know that there is a God and that I – *we* — will be all right. I am not sure that I can feel this, *know* this, with the same certainty as my father.

At least not right now.

But there *is* something BIG in my head and I do not know what it is. My mind is blank. It is just the moment — right now — and it then it comes to me: There is a voice in my mind telling me this is not *just* for me; reminding me that in the midst of the darkest moments I was still okay.

I hear the voice in my mind say, "Live in the moment! Celebrate this very moment."

I am watching Joe as if in slow motion. I see him getting better; he's moving his body, laughing and giggling. Does he know? Does he understand what's happened? Does he worry about the future? Does he understand what all this means to us?

How can he giggle like that? He was — *is* — so brave! Right now is all that he has. It's all he knows. I wonder if I can learn how to do that too? Do all small children live that way? I think so. When did I forget about living that way? When did I lose that skill? I don't know. I have so many questions, so many thoughts. I remember knowing as a child that there were few things to worry about and *all* things to experience, explore and enjoy.

A hurricane, $500 and an old truck

Sometimes it's hard to see opportunity, especially when it seems like the shit has hit the fan! We were just three weeks home from the hospital when the weatherman began to report a storm out in the Lesser Antilles. It meant nothing to me. Propped up in bed, we were watching a lot of TV as a way to pass the time while Joe recovered. Not long after the first report it seemed the storm was getting larger, large enough to be named. I still wasn't aware of what it all meant. There was talk of a hurricane. Having never experienced one before, I really had no idea that I should be the tiniest bit concerned. Then the phone rang. It was the nurse who had been coming by to check on Joe every day.

"You *have* to leave the Keys, Mrs. Hoagland!"

"What? What do you mean? We just got home?"

She asks me if I have a "plan."

"A plan?"

"If you don't have a place to go I will notify the authorities to take you to a shelter. If the storm is bad there might not be any medical response or help available should you need it. The county will announce an emergency evacuation order and then you will have to leave."

"Okay," I said, feeling pretty sure she was overreacting.

When Pete came home he began boarding up the house. He worked all day and night and into the next day securing everything he could. By now I was up to speed and watching the news on TV (Not knowing the station I was watching was the one that most loved to report on and exaggerate impending disasters. But it's probably a good thing I was watching that station then!) The anchorman reported that this huge storm was expected to hit and have a major impact on Miami! Peter had already decided that evacuating to the fish farm was the best thing we could do. He said we would be safe there and, as manager, he could help watch over everything.

I was thinking that sounded like a pretty good idea. I suggested to Kate that she pack a little suitcase with some games and things that she would want to have with her. Kate got busy and proudly reported that she was "on the job!" By 11:00 that night the storm had taken a turn and my "new best friend," the anchorman (At least I felt like we were friends, as I had been glued to the television watching him for a day and a half.), said the storm was coming closer to the Keys than originally expected. All I could think about were the alligators looking for high ground and the science-fiction bugs out at the farm, just waiting to suck on our fresh blood.

After some conversation, Pete and I decided it would be much better to go back to Jupiter to be closer to my father and our other friends, as far away as possible from this storm named *Andrew*.

We loaded the car with dogs, the cat and anything else we could think to bring — including a large trunk Kate had packed — and fled to safe ground, feeling a little bit like the folks from the TV sitcom *The Beverly Hillbillies*, with Granny in her rocking chair on the back of the pickup. I still couldn't understand the big deal about some wind and rain. It was a good thing I had no idea what a hurricane of this strength was about; my anxiety would have been out of control. In Jupiter we decided that rather than crashing with my dad or with our friends, we would stay in our old house which had not yet sold. It was empty, as our renters had just moved out. We borrowed some air mattresses and began to get comfortable in our old surroundings. When everyone started to get hungry I realized I had not even thought about bringing food.

Then Kate announced, "Kate to the rescue!"

She, too, had been watching the television and listening to more than just where the storm was tracking. She heard the advice about what to bring along, and now I understood the trunk. It was filled to the top with food, pots and pans, a can opener, games, candles and flashlights. We had a fun time. Thank goodness Kate had been "on the job." She even thought to pack the champagne I bought to celebrate our anniversary.

The next day's news reported on the disaster. The Florida Keys were "destroyed." They made it sound like the Keys probably didn't exist anymore. Many roads were closed. Cutler Ridge, Homestead and Florida City lay in ruins. Pete was worried about the fish farm. He could not reach any of the people he worked with. Phone lines and many cell towers were down or clogged with all the people trying to use them at the same time. He got in his truck and said he would call once he arrived and could report on the situation. The kids and I went to my father's apartment thinking it was easier to stay there than to continue camping out in our empty house.

[137]

Hours later the phone rang. "It's unbelievable, Deens. There are no trees, no signs on the roads. It's hard to tell where I am. The farm is gone. Completely gone! I can't see the office — the building is not here. The fish are all dead — seventy-thousand pounds of fish, ready for harvesting — all dead!"

I borrowed some money and, armed with a list of the building supplies Pete needed, I found an open Home Depot. I left the children with friends and packed the car with food and lots of drinking water and the supplies.

"I'm going with you!" my father exclaimed.

"No, Dad, this is no place for an old man. I'm concerned for your safety. You might not be able to walk around easily and I have to bring these things to Pete. I promise I will be back by nightfall, but in order to do that I have to leave right now."

The next thing I knew he was buckled into the passenger seat, declaring, "I'm going with you! I'm an old man and I have never seen anything like this. I want to see it. It's history. I promise I won't be a problem."

"You are as stubborn as a mule."

But glad for the company, we set off on another adventure. As we got closer to Miami, we began to see evidence of the strong winds. Most of the street signs had been blown down. The roads were completely empty except for National Guard trucks loaded with men holding guns across their laps in full combat gear and uniform. The closer we got to Homestead there were fewer houses, signs and trees to be seen. Exiting the highway we began to see people walking around in a daze, holding children in their arms, just walking. The streets were strewn with debris. Parts of buildings lay in the streets. Everything was leveled. It was unimaginable. By this time I was thinking there would be nothing left of our house either. Our house was only 30 minutes away from this scene of destruction.

"It's just too much to think about, Dad."

In his way, and *only* his way, he said, "So you should wait and see what God has in his plan for you now. You will see there is always a plan."

There was a long line of people in the street just ahead of us. As we got closer we could see they were waiting in line for food and water. I was lost in thought, thinking about how sad and frightening it was for everyone.

"Stop the car!" Dad shouted suddenly.

"What?" I asked, as if woken from a dream.

He repeated, "Stop the car!"

"Why? What for? It's dangerous here."

I was wondering what he saw. What's going on?

"Stop the car. I'm hungry!"

At the time, I was irritated with him, but now I think it's funny. My father, this old Jewish man who only ate kosher food, was instructing me to stop the car for a hot dog! He must have been desperately hungry. I refused to stop and told him I would get him something to eat as soon as we got to the farm. He pouted the rest of the trip. If he were here today I would ask him if he had really been hungry or had he just wanted to talk to the people and experience standing in that line. I'm not sure. I can't imagine him even taking one bite of those hot dogs.

Pete was right; the farm was destroyed. It took months to clean up. When finally we were able to drive the rest of the way to Key Largo we fully expected to find our house destroyed. But it was as if someone had drawn a line down the road. On one side of the road there was not a tree to be seen, completely barren. The other side of the road – our side — was exactly as we had left it!

I was amazed to see the orchids still hanging in our trees, just as they had been when we left. We had twelve people living in our house for some time until they could get their lives sorted out and back on track. I was doing laundry from sunrise to sunset each day. Compared to so many people, we knew we were fortunate. A tent city was constructed where Homestead Air Force Base once stood. I volunteered my time, providing counseling to the children and families living there. It was a while before school began again and a long time before any sense of normalcy returned for our neighbors just 30 minutes down the road. Luckily for us, and for Fonzie and his friends, our homes were spared. As soon as we were all back home in Key Largo, Joe begged me to take him to see Fonzie! When Fonzie heard Joe's footsteps he popped up from the water, looking around for his friend as well!

Peter worked hard to get the fish farm back up and running, but in the end the odds were against it. He had put his heart and soul into that place. When the board of directors let him go he was heartbroken. I found him sitting in a chair at home, his face blank. His father had died suddenly from a heart attack at age 49, after the stress of his company folding had proved too much for him. My mind went to that place — the place that says history repeats itself. This was more stress than either of us could bear. It felt like another hurricane, but this time it *did* hit our house and our souls too. We were gathering our thoughts, as if that was all we had left. It seemed impossible that so much could've happened in such a short time. Once again we were starting over. But you don't get to pass "Go," and you don't collect $200. We were not playing Monopoly. This was real life. Our life.

It was then that Lloyd asked me again to create a full-time therapy program. "There are so many requests for help now."

"But, Lloyd, I don't have any money to start this."

"We will help you!"

He decided not to charge rent for offices or classrooms. He said he would help us get started in any way that he could.

I went home that night and at dinner explained everything Lloyd and I had discussed. I told Kate, Joe and Pete, "I've thought about doing this for a long time. I'm feeling pulled between my private practice and volunteering with people at Dolphins Plus. In my heart I know that I want to work with the dolphins and children and families. I'm afraid if I get old and pass this up I will have a lot of regret that I didn't try doing this."

[141]

Now that Lloyd had suggested he would help, I saw a way to succeed. "Taking this on will mean less money coming in, less time for us. It will be hard work too."

What I love about our family is how dedicated we are to one another. We are Team Hoagland, and our team agreed to give it a try. That decided, we moved the project forward.

"You know about business," I said to Pete. "I don't know anything about business. I know children and families and what they need. At least help me get started?"

"Okay," he said. "But I can only help until I find another job. We're gonna need a paycheck."

Buckets of fish and helping children

There were so many things that needed to be done and supplies we needed to buy. With Pete not working we were beginning to worry about where the money was going to come from. We knew it would be awhile before we would have a steady income from the dolphin program. We had sold our house in Colorado, but that money and the money we had inherited from my mother's passing were dwindling. We had been so lucky to have had that to get us by all this time. But our bank account was getting close to bottoming out.

By that time, Dad and Pearl were a constant and they decided to get married. I wasn't real happy about it, but what are you going to do? Once again, I told myself that he hadn't agreed with many of my choices in life, but had respected them, so I needed to do the same for him. I decided that during our next visit I would ask him for advice and financial help to get started.

"I have to do this, Dad. I cannot get to your age, look back and wonder, 'What if . . . ?'"

He wrote a check for $500, slipped it into my hand and said, "So when this doesn't work, promise me you'll get a *real* job. You have a sick kid who needs you. You need to look hard at this, get some reality, get a grip on a future that will take care of you."

"I promise, Dad. But I have to try. I want you to see it and believe in it. Look how it helped us. It will help others too. You'll see."

At that time I had an acquaintance from a women's business club. We often sat together during club meetings and enjoyed each other's company. She knew about Joe, about my volunteer work at Dolphins Plus and we had worked together on fundraisers for the children's hospital. Her name is Charlotte and she was a loan officer at a local bank. It was worth a shot I thought. I made an appointment with her. I was nervous. My hands were sweating. What if she, like my father, thought my ideas were ridiculous? Lloyd didn't. Pete didn't. And lots of other people that had seen it believed in it too. But so far none of them believed in it enough to put money into it. Sitting in front of her at the bank was certainly different than sitting beside her at the women's club meetings. Containing my nerves, keeping my calm and professionalism as best I could, I shared my ideas about creating a therapy program working with the dolphins.

[143]

"It will be a not-for–profit organization."

She asked a lot of questions. I had the answers she needed and she seemed impressed with the idea.

"Well," she said, "we just need to figure out what you can use as collateral so you have the funds you need to get started. But before the bank can make any loan it has to be a legally established not-for-profit."

She referred me to a local attorney who she said was quite generous and might help with its incorporation. I phoned and requested his next available appointment. Once in his office I was even more worried than I had been with Charlotte. This is a way-out idea. He knows nothing about me. Why would he think this was a good idea and want to help? I told myself I had to try. I was ushered into a boardroom dominated by a large table. He motioned for me to sit down.

"How can I help you?"

"I'm Deena Hoagland. I'm a clinical social worker," telling him my credentials so that he would know from the outset that I was a professional.

"I am also a mother — the mother of a very special young man who has had to face incredible obstacles in his life thus far."

Once I began to tell him the story about Joe, how we got to Key Largo, Joe's stroke and meeting Fonzie, I do not think I stopped or came up for air. Not once. I was so nervous, I was afraid if I looked at him I would begin to cry. I didn't want him to see me become emotional. I did not want him to view me as fragile. I kept my head down until I had finished.

"So that is what brought me to you. I was told you were kind and generous and that you might help me incorporate as a not-for-profit organization."

One big sigh, one breath more and then I looked up at him from across the table and realized he had been crying. That moment I knew life was about to change again.

"You had me in the first few minutes, Mrs. Hoagland. It would be my pleasure to help you."

Back in Charlotte's office we struggled to find a way for the bank to agree to loan us some money. Finally she asked, "What about your car? Do you owe any money on it?"

"No. We don't owe any money, but it is old, sometimes it won't start and it has over 200,000 miles on it!"

"Never mind all that," she said "let me check its Blue Book value."

Moments later she returned smiling.

"How will $5,000 do?"

With that and the money from my father, we purchased a computer and a fax machine and printed our first applications to the program. Island Dolphin Care was born! If this did not work we would have to move on to another career, just as I had promised my father.

Lloyd had saved many of the addresses and contact information from the multitude of letters and phone calls we had received from people inquiring about therapy programs for their family members, so Peter and I began with the fax machine in our bedroom. We mailed applications to 500 of the names on Lloyd's list and waited. We decided we could begin with two families per week and if we had more requests we would have to hire another therapist to help. To our surprise and delight the fax machine was ringing through all hours of the day and night! Before we knew it we had our first clients.

Joe's neurologist was excited too. He was anxious to see if this could help others in the same way it had helped Joe. He, along with other local professionals, including the lawyer who had been so generous and an accountant friend of Joe's visiting nurse, joined our board of directors. Each of them helped us get the educational tools and supplies we needed to begin the program. It was not long after we began that I was able to walk proudly into the bank and pay off the loan Charlotte had helped with.

We were soon exploding with requests. There were many families who called wanting to participate but didn't have the funds they needed. We researched grants but with little success. It was when my friend Lisa called that everything changed. She had read an article in *The Miami Herald* about a foundation offering assistance to programs that worked with children with disabilities. I called them immediately. A woman named Louise answered. She said she was the executive director.

When I explained who I was, what I was doing and what I needed, she immediately said, "I wish I could help you, dear. Your program sounds just wonderful. But our foundation only assists programs in Miami, as well as families with children that reside in Miami. I wish you all the luck in the world!"

I responded quickly, "But many of the families that want to attend our program *live* in Miami! What difference does it make where the program is?"

There was a bit of irritation in her voice as she responded, "I'm very busy. Our board of directors sets the regulations. Perhaps I can suggest that you call this gentleman that I know. I think he might be of some assistance to you!"

I thought she just wanted to get me off the phone; I had pissed her off, had been too pushy. I took his number. Sitting at my desk looking at the number, I found myself dialing it. What did I have to lose anyway? All he could do was say "No." By the third ring I wasn't feeling hopeful. When he answered I was somewhat lost in thought and taken off guard.

"Yes, can I help you?"

I explained that Louise had referred me. He asked a few questions and sounded a bit uninterested. Then in an attempt to end the conversation he explained that he was on his way to the Florida Keys for the weekend.

"Perhaps we can speak on Monday morning?"

I responded excitedly, "We live in Key Largo! Would you like to have a meeting? See the facility? Meet the dolphins?"

I thought I was about to jump out of my skin. Maybe he thought I was too excited. Perhaps that is what interested him.

"Okay. That sounds like a good idea."

We made plans to meet for dinner that night. I kept playing it over and over in my mind — he said it was a good idea! I could not wait to tell Peter. We met later that evening at a local fish joint. It was a place that I thought was unpretentious and quiet. His name is Jordan. I thought he was one of the most intelligent people I had ever met. In fact, there were times that I found myself nodding; pretending I understood what he was saying, but not wanting him to think I was stupid! He wanted to see the facility and offered to meet us there the next day. After our next meeting he nonchalantly suggested that he would assist us for six months at no cost, *but* I had to agree to do everything he asked me to do and exactly the way he told me to do it. He said that in six months' time he would raise enough funding to pay his salary as well as a salary for ourselves.

He added, "I want to be clear that I am not going to do the work. I am just going to tell you what to do and how to do it! The rest, Baby, is up to you!"

Well how could we possibly go wrong with that? Jordan was our hope. He was brilliant; so much so that I was afraid I would fail because I didn't understand what he was asking me to do a lot of the time! I decided that no matter how stupid I told myself I was, I would be brave enough to ask him to explain everything until I *did* understand. This not-for-profit world was one I did not comprehend very well. I was frightened; but at the same time, excited! The way things were going now, we could not fail!

[148]

Jordan was a huge help. We wrote numerous grants to help fund programs for families who could not afford to pay on their own.

By this time we had grown to working with eight families each week. We hired special education teachers to help us provide the programs. Children with illnesses and disabilities came from all over the world. Island Dolphin Care was making a difference in people's lives and the dolphins were a very big part of it. Many people speculated that it was because of the dolphins' echolocation. I suppose, to be perfectly honest, I thought that, too, at first. But if it was due to echolocation, then why do some children and their families not change at all? We could argue that not all medications or treatments work for all people. To me it was more than that. As time went by I began to realize the real reasons.

When a child has a disability or illness, the shock and pain for a family is huge. No one can plan for an event like that. The loss is deep. Finding answers is often difficult and overwhelming. There is no instruction book, not for family members or friends. I am talking about the ones we read when we have our first baby. I looked for one in 1986. There was not a single book around about what to do when the sky falls and a child is diagnosed with a rare disorder, illness or disability. I watched in the waiting rooms as some people found help in prayer. I watched some find the answers with their doctors or with the medications and treatments. When those things work, it's wonderful.

But for families like ours, families with devastating blows that don't seem to end, the answers are hard to come by and far and few between. What happened to us, and what happens all too often to others, is that sadness creeps in. It creeps in so slowly, insidiously, that it's barely noticed. It has moved right in before you realize it. That happened to me. No one noticed. We were too busy running for Joe's life — for the next breath. We did not have time for joy in our lives. We never even thought about joy. We were too busy coping. No one is at fault. We did not think about it. We did not have the time. I certainly did not think about it and I'm a professional. Our culture trains us to think that medicine is the only cure; that it's what we need in times like these. If you are sick, stay in bed, stay home — don't go out and don't do things! But that becomes lonely and isolating. Consumed daily with nightmares, fear and anxiety, the reality of it all is overpowering.

What I found in the dolphins was the smile I had lost; the relationship with my children as *Mommy*, not nurse; the laughter with my husband, daughter and son. I reclaimed myself and my family with a dose of joy. It is that joy which empowered all of us to move forward and provided the energy we needed to cope with the obstacles we faced — obstacles beyond our control, obstacles we could not change. Joy became the glue that held us together in times of distress.

There are programs for children with special needs. I worked at one a long time ago. It's a fact of life that most

[150]

parents have to work to pay the medical bills, often finding themselves in financial crisis. They may not get the chance to work side-by-side with therapists and teachers, observing and learning how to help their child. Often the child attends a program and goes home at the end of the day to a family that does not have the opportunity to speak with the teachers and therapists to learn how to be helpful at home, and siblings all too often live lives separated from one another because they are involved in different activities. There are fewer opportunities to interact as a family. Parents are so consumed with worry and getting through the day's tasks that by the end of the day they're exhausted.

We wanted Island Dolphin Care to provide for others the therapeutic and educational tools that we had needed but did not have available. Surely if we experienced these needs, so did others. The impact of the program for families was and is enormous.

Suddenly families and children find themselves smiling and laughing in the paradise offered by Island Dolphin Care and the Florida Keys. Parents watch their children play, interact differently and experience success. Children gain self-esteem, as Joe did. Family members are included in all sessions and have the opportunity to learn side-by-side with the therapists who teach the most current and innovative techniques. Teaching is presented as play because play is what children know how to do and want to do. It's not scary, it's fun. It's a therapeutic vacation for everyone — a vacation most families with a differently-abled child could not have ever dreamed of taking. Island Dolphin

Care is a place to meet others like themselves. Word of mouth spread quickly and more and more families wanted to come and join the program.

Not long after we were beginning to relax and celebrate the success of the program, I noticed Lloyd touring the facilities with people who were clearly not clients. I finally had the courage to ask him what was going on.

"I've been doing this a long time," he said. "I'm getting older and I want to sell the facility. The people I've been showing around are interested buyers."

"Oh, my God! NO! They will never let me keep doing this. What can I do to stop this?"

Lloyd looked at me in an understanding way and said simply, "Well, I guess you have the choice to buy it yourself."

YIKES! I 'm thinking, but I say to him, "That's ridiculous. You know I have no money."

"Well," he said, "I can't tell you anything more than that."

That night I could not think of anything else. When I called the board of directors the next day they all said "Well, let's buy it then." The attorney said he would draw up a letter of intent to buy.

"Deena, if we do not have the money in 90 days there is no loss, but at least we can say we tried."

When I presented Lloyd with the letter he smiled.

"Now you're talking, Kiddo."

But the looming and dooming fact was that I had to raise the money in just 90 days!

[152]

George, my new teacher

There are people on this earth who come here on a mission. They accomplish all they intend to and make a difference for the world. And when they leave, the world is a better place. I was fortunate to have had the incredible honor and experience of meeting George B. To me he was a man larger than life.

Back then I used to pick up the newspaper and read about him. He had contributed to rebuilding the Miami Zoo after Hurricane Andrew demolished it. On his birthday there was a photo of him with a leopard by his side. So, I said to myself, it's time to write him a letter. I really didn't expect an answer, or maybe I did? But I wrote a letter. A few days later, Jordan told me that I should phone George and invite him to swim with the dolphins. To my surprise and delight, he accepted. He arrived in a chauffeured limousine. I was frightened, but I had done things like this before and they had worked in my favor. I decided that no matter what happened, I would ask for his help. After all, I thought he was someone who could make the difference we needed now.

During his swim, George laughed loudly. In his bathing suit and without the limo he looked like any other man. I could tell he was intrigued with the dolphins. I also knew he would not have come if he was not interested in what I was doing.

After the swim, standing by the lagoon overlooking the dolphins, he said, "Deena, I would like to help you . . . BUT . . . (Long pause) you don't have experience. I don't know you. I do not get involved with projects that might fail. So

[153]

before I get involved you have to prove to me that you are serious and that you can be successful. This is a test. I will give you $250,000 but only after you raise $250,000. One way or another we will both learn how successful and serious you really are."

Within the 90-day time limit, we worked hard and raised the $250,000. George kept his promise to provide the matching funds. This enabled us to enter into an agreement with Lloyd to purchase half his physical property and four dolphins — of course, Fonzie being one of them. The most important things to know are: 1. We were successful, 2. George was always available whenever I needed his advice and 3. I did everything exactly the way Jordan told me to. We became so successful that within six months we had to hire more staff to help us. They were then, and still are, wonderfully dedicated people who have contributed a great deal of heart, soul and knowledge. They are the bricks and mortar of what Island Dolphin Care is today.

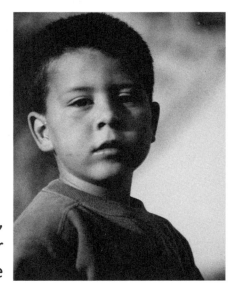

Joe,
shortly after
his stroke

The kids
loved their
Grandpa
Manny

Feeding Fonzie, with assistance from the dolphin trainer

Joe, standing on his own at last, to feed Fonzie

Joe, with Lloyd

Joe,
playing ball
with Fonzie

[159]

The foyer at Island Dolphin Care

One of the classrooms

The touch tank

Me,
with Kate and Joe
(Fonzie is on the right)

Joe and Pete,
with their
handmade
surfboards

Joe,
surfing in
Costa Rica

The future belongs
to those who believe
in the beauty of their dreams.

~ attributed to Eleanor Roosevelt

Part Three: *Accolades, Hang Ten, Accept the Journey*

Sitting in the bleachers

Kate, Pete and I are sitting in the bleachers, anxious to watch Joe walk down the aisle to collect his diploma with everyone else in his class. The thought in my head is so loud I'm sure others can hear it: "Cross off another 'Never'!" Joe is beaming as he comes down the aisle. Scanning the crowd for us, our eyes meet and he waves. We are so incredibly proud. I pinch myself to make sure this is not a dream; that we are really here. The award part of the ceremony begins and many of his peers are receiving scholarships and high honors. A few teachers approach the podium and one begins to speak. I have known him for many years.

He begins by saying, "This award is my favorite, especially this year. This award is teacher-nominated. It is The Best of the Class Award for 2005. When the faculty came together to discuss the qualifications of whomever would be chosen for this award, I did not have to think long about it. I knew immediately the student I had chosen. Usually this results in a long meeting and sometimes a heated discussion among the faculty. That did not happen this year. There was little discussion because we were all in agreement. In fact, the only heated part of our discussion was over which one of us would be presenting this award. We could not agree, so tonight there are three of us presenting the award."

I was thinking, Wow, this is really cool. This kid's parents will be so proud. This is the best award of the evening. The next teacher comes to the podium:

"I have learned to become a better teacher because of this student. This student came to me at the end of last school year asking to be allowed in my class. I said, 'No. It's a tough class. You won't be able to keep up.' He asked for a chance. He said, 'Please don't judge me. If I don't keep up I will drop it after the first semester and give another student the chance.' So I relented and let him in my class."

He continues, "I am not sure which one of us learned more this year — him or me, but I know that I became a better teacher."

The third teacher approaches the podium and simply says, "This year, this award goes to a student who never gave up, one who had a smile for everyone every day, one who offers help, hope and compassion for others and, above all, teaches us that *anything* is possible, if you just have patience and the strong will to succeed."

My heart is pounding as he announces, "Joe Hoagland, will you please come up to the podium and claim this award!"

And with that, everyone in the auditorium is on their feet, clapping and cheering. Kate, Pete and I are wiping tears of joy.

Joe received a full scholarship to marine mechanics school. It's there that he decides to take a class in fiberglass and asks his teacher if it is all right to build a surfboard for his final project.

[166]

Mamarazzi

There is a special place. A place that Pete had dreamed of but thought it might be just a hope, a wish, a dream. I am the only one on the beach. It is a beautiful day. The air seems to wrap me in a blanket of comfort. I can't believe that I am standing here, camera in hand, and no one else is with me to see this. But I have my camera and the photos will tell the story.

They are on their boards facing each other. I can see that they are talking. I wonder are they talking about — the waves, the day? Is Pete telling Joe what to do? They worked on those boards for months, shaping them together in the garage, choosing the paint and creating the logo: "You Don't Know Jack" (with a photo of our dog, Jack, in the middle). And we are here on this beautiful morning ready for the test run — ready to *hang ten*.

The wave comes and I pick up the camera, ready to get the photo, to capture this amazing moment. Suddenly out of nowhere, I hear a voice. "Excuse me," a man says, standing next to me, "but are you all right?"

Wiping away some of the happiest tears of my life, I choke trying to get the words out, "Yes!" He's looking at me perplexed now. I'm sure he must think I'm crazy.

"Those are my guys out there waiting for the right wave, a wave they never thought they could ride together. There is a story about three pages of 'Nevers' and we just crossed off another one!" I let the tears go, put the camera to my eyes and get the shot.

[167]

Post-traumatic stress

I can hear my heart pounding and wonder if the people around me can hear it too. I wonder if they can tell how anxious I am. Patiently sitting in the crowded waiting room, I scan other people's faces and realize they must be feeling anxious too, but for different reasons. I look at Pete and know he can probably hear my heart beating, because I know he feels it too. The couples sitting across from us are young, all the women pregnant. None of them would be in this room if there wasn't reason for concern.

I look over at Kate and she looks to me for reassurance. I try as best I can to smile and appear strong. It's her first baby and because of our history her doctor advised her to have a fetal echocardiogram to make sure the baby is developing normally, the heart free of defects. Her name is called and we walk the long hallway to the examining room. The nurse is friendly and cheerful as she shows Kate to her gown and table. I have not said one word. I guess I have been concentrating on keeping up appearances.

I don't want her to know what I'm feeling. After all, I'm here to support her. But it all comes back — the antiseptic smell, the long corridors, the glaring lights and cheerful smiles pretending nothing is wrong. The nurse begins by applying the warm lotion to her belly and I cannot take my eyes off the monitor. By now I know exactly what I'm looking at — having seen it so many times before. Pete waits in the hallway. While Kate is getting dressed, I join Peter just outside the door. He takes my hand and squeezes hard. A door down the hall opens and a couple emerges. They are holding hands, eyes swollen from crying. Pete squeezes my hand again and we sigh, understanding that they have received unwelcome news. It was weird; as though we were looking back and seeing ourselves walking down that hall. Kate appears and we are ushered into another room where the radiologist will meet with us. He enters the room smiling and then I know he will tell her that everything is as it should be. The baby is growing strong and healthy. We leave happy, and feeling relieved, go to lunch.

It's not until we are lying safely in bed that night, holding one another, that we have the chance to talk about it: our moment of post-traumatic stress in the medical center hallway hoping, of course, that Kate couldn't see or feel our pain — the pain of remembering.

It's not until Henry turns two and she is pregnant with her second child that she calls one day to say, "Mom, I don't know how you did it. I look at Henry and realize that if anything ever happened to him I would die. I wouldn't be able to cope. I don't know how you and dad managed. You amaze me."

Maybe she understood before that day, but I'm certain she gets it now.

In search of the elusive blue butterfly

It was an ordinary day. We were taking a drive up the mountain looking for the Black Sheep Bar. Peter said he heard it had an amazing view and great music at night. We could use a little break from the sun and surf, so an adventure in the afternoon was just what we needed. As we climbed the dirt road the trees and wildflowers changed. The dirt on the mountainside is red and wet from the recent rain — I was immediately reminded of our road in Kittredge. I can't remember the last time I had thought about that road. Although this is a tropical environment, there are many similarities. The sun is shining and Pete is having a great time in four-wheel drive, taking the winding turns higher and higher up the mountain.

There's not another car or person in sight. As we climb, I think of our mountaintop — the place we loved and left so quickly, not knowing that we were embarking on a new life. I am in awe of every detail — the flowers, the trees, the ferns and the dew on the leaves. We come around a big curve. For a second I blink and I know that the movement is the same. This could be the last turn of our dirt road; it feels exactly the same. But it's not. We arrive at the top and our house is not there — just an empty lot with an amazing view. We get out to take in the scenery and I walk over to the edge for a better look. There, sitting on a leaf, is a blue butterfly! I have never seen this color blue! How beautiful it is! It takes flight and we both admire it. I think how stupid that I don't have my camera! How could I leave the house without it? On the way back down the mountain the views are perfect and vast. The blue butterflies alight in front of the car, on the side of the road, and just for a moment we are able to sit in awe of its unusual beauty and flight, skipping, fluttering from bush to bush.

[170]

I think we will have to come back up here to see this view again and maybe I can take a photo of this blue butterfly. When Joe arrives with some friends we decide to take them up the mountain. I tell them about the blue butterfly and how much I want a photo of it, so we all keep our eyes peeled, intently searching for the blue butterfly. When we reach the mountaintop there they are in flight before us! We're all shouting: "There it is! . . . Quick, there now! . . . There!" I try to catch the perfect shot, but no matter how hard I try it eludes me. We laugh again and again. Delicately they fly, fluttering in every direction, eluding me.

On the way down the mountain we are laughing and talking, and I say, "That's it! That is what all of us are doing — searching for the elusive butterfly. We catch sight of her; we try to keep her, memorialize her in a photo forever, but no matter how hard we try she eludes us. Her fragile beauty cannot be captured. It is only something to be experienced, talked about, held in the heart and, in an instant, she is gone. In just one breath."

It is what it is — just perfect.

Pillow talk

I look around, still in thought.
I think: This is my life — one breath.
I'm dreaming: Jessica, one of the dolphins, is on my pillow again. She is telling me something and I am trying to

listen, to pay attention so that I can remember everything when I wake up.

This is what I remember: She is saying,

"It is the ocean, the sky, the moon, the sun, one breath . . . We are connected by one breath."

I see myself standing in Kittredge watching the trees bend. Aspens dance and glisten; I'm listening to the wind in the trees. I am feeling light and happy. She tells me to look all around, to pay attention!

"You are not to wander now."

Okay, I say, and I smile at her.

She points.

The leaves turn brown.

They fall. They die.

The earth changes.

So do we.

One breath at a time; I tell her I understand.

I had to let parts of us go to let another part grow. She shows me a tree that loses a limb and another leaf that falls.

I hear myself saying, "If I had known I might have been able to welcome the changes instead of being afraid when they came."

I can't tell if I am still dreaming.

I awake. I am drenching wet! Was I sweating? I'm disoriented. Am I still sleeping? Dreaming? I don't exactly know. I look around and see him asleep next to me.

The only thing that I know for sure today is Peter. For 40 years we have been waking up next to each other. We share this incredible life and incredible love. I see his eyes

[172]

open. The lines in his face that surround his eyes smile. I know for this moment that we have each other. I am so grateful.

I take another breath.

Epilogue

March 21, 2000

It's 9:00 am. The phone rings. Peter answers. I hear the concern in his voice and look up.

"It's your dad, Deens. He died. He was in the front row of synagogue. When prayers ended he did not get up to go to *Kiddush*."

His friend Rueben poked him, "C'mon, Manny, let's go!" thinking he had fallen asleep. I smile, thinking to myself: Even in his death god left him the parking space right in front.

March 11, 2004

Not long after meeting George and writing many successfully funded grants, we knew we needed a new building in which to house our growing programs. I was sitting at my desk writing the grant proposal when our curator came into the office.
It was 7:30 am.

"Hey, Deena, I need to talk to you about something."

Barely looking up I answered, "Okay, maybe later. I'm almost done with this proposal and can't stop right now."

He didn't leave.

"We *really* need to talk."

A little concerned by his tone, I looked up to see his face. No words yet telling me if we have a problem.

"Okay, what's wrong?"

He begins. Then there it is . . . the one breath.

"There is no good way to say this. I am so sorry, but Fonzie has passed away."

I ran over the lagoon bridge in disbelief, as if the words had not been spoken. Maybe I did not hear him right! But in my heart I knew the truth. I was just not ready. I sat on the dock waiting and hoping for him to pop up as he always did. But there below me lay his still body. Pete immediately went to school to get Joe. Everyone knew Joe had to be there, had to see for himself. Not one person suggested otherwise. When Joe arrived we sat on the dock and cried together. We watched as another dolphin, Squirt, and the trainers helped bring him to the surface. It was dramatic — I was sure of that. There is no other way it could have been. Fonzie was taken for a necropsy. The law required it. When the results came back the vet explained that Fonzie had a heart defect! Maybe that is why, when he was first discovered, he was alone. Maybe he was not able to keep up with his pod. Maybe he was weak and unable to hunt as well as the others. Maybe that is why he was so hungry that he took fish from them right away. We had so many questions.

We sat on the stairs to the bridge and talked. When the vet had finished explaining, Joe looked up with eyes full of sorrow.

"So, it's true. It's really true. Fonzie *chose* me. He knew we were alike."

The moment it sunk in, Joe was inconsolable. He was having difficulty letting go. I made arrangements for Fonzie's ashes to be placed in a large salt urn, which would dissolve when placed in the ocean. A close friend offered his boat, large enough to accommodate 50 people, to bring Fonzie's ashes to the open ocean. Joe was still insisting that he couldn't go with us to say his final goodbye. On the day we were to pick up Fonzie's ashes, I asked Joe to accompany me. With the top down on our funky old convertible, I placed the urn on Joe's lap and buckled them both in for the drive to the boat. It was a beautiful evening. Wiping tears from his face, I said tenderly, "You know Fonzie always wanted to ride in a convertible. Don't you think he enjoys the feeling of the wind in his hair?" We laughed the rest of the way to the boat. Perhaps it was remembering the giggles that we so often shared with Fonzie that enabled Joe to carry on.

Accompanied by Joe, all his other friends and the family that loved and adored him, Fonzie's ashes were taken out to the blue waters where the wild dolphins play.

June 25, 2004

It's 9:00 pm when the phone rings. It's Billy, the night watchman.

"Deena?"

"Yes, Billy, is everything okay?"

"Sure is! I think you better come down here though. I see a little tail! Squirt is about to have her calf!"

Shortly after 9:00 pm we sat on the steps of the bridge separating Island Dolphin Care from Dolphins Plus and in the light of a crescent moon we watched as Fiji — Fonzie's last gift to us — entered the world.

November, 2011

Joe is turning 25. He lives independently. He has a great life. He has great friends. He still gives the best tours at Island Dolphin Care. He is our hero and still, so often, one of my teachers.

Every once in a while, I wish I could reach for the phone and have my parents answer. I wish I could tell them — tell them everything worked out just the way it should. And on that day when, at five years old, I said with such conviction that one day I would grow up to take care of children and animals, somehow I knew it to be true. I just had no idea how I was going to get there.

I want to tell my father that every day I get an email that reminds me of our talks together. It is an inspirational reading from the Kabbalah Centre International that comes to my email daily. I want to read him part of today's message, a quote from Yehuda Berg:

> *June 26th Weekly Tune-Up: . . . "Each of us comes into this world with our* tikkun *('correction'). But on some level, in a parallel universe, our*

[178]

*correction has already been perfected. Our
spiritual work is to remove our* klipot, *the shells
of negativity, so we can borrow from our
perfected self.*

*Rabbi Rav Brandwein, my father's teacher,
explains that 'borrow from' means to call upon
our inner strength and certainty to help us
accomplish whatever seems impossible. Every
single one of us will eventually achieve this
perfection, whether it takes one incarnation or
one-hundred incarnations.*

*Accomplishment relies on us knowing we are
perfect just the way we are. Of course we should
always be open to facing uncomfortable truths
about ourselves and changing accordingly. But
it's important to be aware of the perfection in our
lives.*

*Have you ever survived a difficult period only to
later realize that the whole journey worked out
exactly the way it was supposed to? Kabbalists
say this is because perfection is always within us.
It is the spark of God. Many religions put God out
there as an all-powerful force. But the Zohar says
No! The all-powerful force that wants to give us
all of the fulfillment in the world is inside each
one of us.*

Our goal is to live from this place. But this requires a shift in consciousness: It requires surrendering the part of us that says, for whatever reason, 'I can't do it.' It's the part of you that thinks you are alone in your struggle.

You are not alone. You've got a pretty special person in there with you. It's that 'you' that likes to go the extra mile, share and think about other people's feelings first, and love without strings attached. You have added support for tapping into the version of yourself that has passed every test. Use this time to make great improvements in your relationships, your work situation, your health and every part of your life that calls out for transformation."

— from Wisdom Blogs: www.kabbalah.com

Afterword

Somehow I stumbled upon ways to face adversity with a smile. As my friend Dyan — she with the "perfect" child — shared with me years later, she watched and marveled as we "made lemonade from lemons." I truly was learning that "circumstances" and "excuses" were really just different words for, and completely different perspectives on, the same turning points in one's life.

I found acceptance in laughter, in appreciating the moment, in the realization that life and nature are so fragile, in the beauty of this incredible friendship — this extraordinary relationship between Joe and a magnificent Atlantic bottlenose dolphin. In the most unlikely place, under the most trying of circumstances, the answers were before me.

THE DOLPHINS

Dolphin dreams, sea-beans and seahorses

Fonzie's favorite activity was for Joe to throw him a sea-bean. Joe loved to find them on the beach by our house, collecting every one he could find for Fonzie. Joe said Fonzie really liked the big ones. We would carry bags of them to him. Joe would throw one to Fonzie and Fonzie would bring it back to Joe and together they would pass it back and forth. Joe knew this game was a left-handed game and in the beginning he struggled to hold onto the bean. Fonzie never minded when Joe would drop it — that was just part of the game — and so back and forth the two played until time to go home.

I loved it whenever we arrived at the facility only to be told we could not play that day because Fonzie had other things on his mind. There were times that the facility would open the gates and allow the dolphins to play in the ocean. Lloyd would say, "Don't worry. They always come back. They just come back when they are ready!" Now and again Fonzie would come back to the gate but remain on the other side. He would just hang out at the gateway. He seemed to enjoy watching the trainers trying to coax him in because they had a plan for the day and having Fonzie in the ocean canal was not part of their plan!

I learned that no matter how hard someone tries to make a dolphin do something, if a dolphin doesn't want to do it there is nothing anyone can do to make them! It was

Fonzie's game, his joke on everyone. Eventually Fonzie would swim into the enclosure, but only when he was ready! I am sure Fonzie has many offspring swimming in the waters near Key Largo! We have just not met them. Once he stayed away for 11 days!

Lloyd's adorable wife, Oma, would watch him from an upstairs window. She would open the window and call to him, "Yoo-Hoo, Fonzie! Hello!"

Every time she did it, the trainers would say, "Oma, he's not a dog! He doesn't know you are calling to him!"

She would flap her hand at them as if to say, "What do you know about Fonzie?" And as if it had been planned — right on time — he would pop his head out of the water, in front of her window, and chortle to her! Oma, Joe and I would laugh and laugh! *

Jessica

I began to have dolphin dreams. Jessica would slide up on my pillow at night. We would be eye to eye.

I would begin with a big sigh, "No, Jessica, I can't go with you tonight. I am so tired."

She would say that we have to go! We have so much to see; there's so much I have to show you.

"Please," she would beg, "just put your hand on my side. I will do the work. You just have to keep your hand on

---

* Due to changes in the Marine Mammal Protection Act, the opening of the facility's ocean gate is no longer allowed.

my side. Come, we do not have much time if I am to bring you back by morning!"

I remember we always began by going through long tunnels, the sides walled with rock. We are swimming — *she* is, my hand stays on her side — the water is warm and we travel far and fast. She takes me many places. I can't remember most of them. What I do remember is her thanking me at dawn when she brings me back. Just before leaving — facing eye to eye — she looks into my heart and thanks me for the journey. I awaken wet around my neck and knees, and wonder: Was I just dreaming, sweating . . . ?

I can't remember.

Squirt

They slide into the water. There she is, right next to her, waiting. Wendy tells Kate to hold onto her dorsal fin.

"Squirt's waiting for you! She's so happy you're here to swim!"

Kate holds on and off they go! Squirt dives, Kate still holding on. I get a little nervous.

"Wendy, where did they go? Will she bring her back?"

"Sure," Wendy says. "Take it easy. They're having fun!"

They fly out of the water on the opposite side of the lagoon! Kate's still holding on! And then another dive down, over and over. It seemed neither would ever get tired.

When finally they do, Kate announces, "If I can do that, Mom, I can do anything!"

Kate is learning to let go of her fears.

Nicky and Dreamer

I am swimming. The dolphins surround me. I am in the middle like a sandwich; one on top of me, one on the bottom. I am the jelly in this dolphin sandwich. I can hardly breathe.

Wendy shouts to me from the side. "Go with it!"

I hear her laughing. My heart swells with love for them. It seems that I can feel their hearts beating! Or is it mine? I do not know. Cradled as I swim, until they are done with me, I surrender to their love.

Dreamer and the ring

My friend is swimming and I am filming so he can keep this memory with him. Funny . . . I think it's funny that people think they can hold a memory on a tape, when the memory is in your heart. I have so many tapes and I never watch them. Maybe that's because I prefer the memory in my heart. I am wondering what other people do?

A man hurriedly climbs on the dock and tells Bobby, the trainer, "I've just lost my wedding ring! I'm on my honeymoon and was diving and the next thing I know the ring slipped off my finger! My wife is swimming there and if she finds out she will be so upset! I don't want to ruin the swim for her!"

I put the camera on pause and set it down. I'm on the dock with them. The man is sitting at the edge of the dock completely distraught. Dreamer comes to take a look. If she were human she might have been saying to them, "Hey,

[186]

Mister, can I help? Is there something wrong?" We all look at her at the same moment and notice she has something in her mouth, pressed within her rostrum.

"Look! Dreamer has your ring!"

And she certainly does! Bobby puts out his hand thinking Dreamer was going to give it to him, but she had another idea. She wants to play a game: Now you see it, now you don't! She shows us the ring and just as we reach for it, she drops it. Then she snatches it up again just before it hits bottom and returns to the surface to show us she still has it. Then she drops it again! This game continued a few more times. Bobby asked the man if he could dive well.

"Yes," the man responds.

"Good," Bobby says. "Keep your eye on the ring and the next time she drops it, dive immediately into the water to get it. You only have one chance at this. As soon as you dive in, she will swim away. Then you have to grab the ring or it will sink to the bottom and we will have one hell of a time trying to find it then!
"Okay? One ... Two ... Three ... DIVE!"

He gets the ring!

Bob and Peter K

Peter K was a teenager with Ewing's sarcoma, a rare and brutal cancer. It was in his leg. After multiple surgeries Peter was having great difficulty walking. It was painful for him to bend his leg or to bear weight on it. He loved sports and he loved to swim. His parents thought swimming with the dolphins would provide motivation for him to move his leg and continue with his treatments and the physical therapy that was so painful. We became close friends because he came often to swim. He had a special friendship with the dolphin named Bob. Like Fonzie with Joe, Bob would find Peter as soon as he entered the water. He would somehow communicate to the other dolphins, "This kid is mine!"

It was a beautiful friendship to watch and it did, in fact, provide Peter the motivation to continue his fight against cancer. Sadly, he lost that fight just before he turned 16. It was during one of our discussions toward the end of his battle that he told me that sometimes swimming with the dolphins was the only thing that provided him comfort or joy, as well as providing an escape from his frightening disease and the constant thoughts of it.

"When I'm in the water swimming with Bob, I'm just Peter swimming with Bob, having fun. I don't feel pain or think about cancer. It's just me and Bob."

I understand that.

I was going through a particularly difficult time then, writing grants that resulted in many rejections and a lack of funds. At times, I was discouraged and thought we might not succeed. This young man made me promise that I would never give up. He said swimming with Bob helped him keep up the fight as long as he could and that it gave him courage, joy and peace of mind when he needed it. At his request, his parents sent us a $5,000 donation after his passing.

Sometimes, when things feel like they are getting too hard to keep Island Dolphin Care going, I remember young

Peter and my promise to him. That promise has kept things moving right along at Island Dolphin Care for a long time now. I keep my promises.

Samantha

I am swimming. It is a beautiful day. I love hearing the dolphins' whistles and squeaks! I wonder what they talk about. I know they are talking to one another. Are they talking to me too? Will I ever know?

I love looking at the coral rock walls. They come to see what I am looking at. We dive, turn, spin and delight in the patterns of the sun shining through the water. I wish I were a better swimmer so that I could swim with them like some of the trainers do, but I am limited. Breathless, I climb out of the water. Sitting on the dock I thank them for our time. Samantha joins me, searching into my eyes and then she spits something at me. I look and to my amazement she has given me a little seahorse! Was she giving me a gift?

Spunky and Duke

Spunky is a large plus-size dolphin. She is a good friend. Her calf's name is Duke. He is adorable. This is her first calf at the facility. She is very protective and keeps him tucked in and close by her at all times. She won't come to the dock when certain people are there and especially when there are strangers. But she knows when I am there and comes to see me. The trainers say it's because she trusts me.

Genie

Genie is one of the most beautiful dolphins I have ever seen. She was slender, yet muscular and long. Her first calf was named Alfonse. His name is a combination of his father's name, Fonzie, and Lloyd's middle name, Al. Genie enjoyed interacting with people. She was friendly, sensitive and generally more serious than the others in her pool. She was one of the older original dolphins from the wild. When she became ill and everyone realized that she was at the end of her life, dying from old age, the staff brought a special above-ground medical pool in which to keep her comfortable. The staff agreed to take turns spending nights with her, never leaving her alone.

This went on for some time. People grew tired, she was tired too; but we knew that her time to leave us was coming soon. Joe wanted to help. He loved Genie. The dolphins have been part of our family now for twenty years. And to all of us they *are* family. Joe went every day to help. He monitored the pool, kept it clean and made sure that the staff had everything they needed, often offering to get them a drink, something to eat or dry towels. When a dolphin dies, it is not any different for any of us than if a friend or family member died. We were there around the clock, day and night.

I came to the side of the pool often to check on how Joe was doing and the rest of the staff, as well as Genie. I thought to myself, how lucky she is to have all of the people that love her surround and hold her until her last breath.

[190]

How lucky we *all* are, as staff, to be able to hold her and say goodbye, and offer our support until her last breath.

Life is so interesting. I have thought about what it must be like to be a dolphin — wished I *was* a dolphin — so many times over the years. They have taught me so much about life. One thing is for sure: dolphins adapt and manage much better than humans do. They hold no grudges, have no past or future and celebrate as the very best each and every moment they have! The days I spent watching the staff take turns holding Genie, supporting her and saying goodbye — and having Joe as a part of that, as a young adult — brought things full circle. As she took her last breath, we cried and thanked her for some of the most wonderful moments in our lives. I can only hope that when it is my time to die that I will also be in the arms of all those who love me.

Beautiful Sarah

She was sick. Was this the end? We sat by her pool feeling helpless and afraid that it might be time to say goodbye to this beautiful old friend. It just might be her time. I watched as her daughter, just three years old, was tucked under her day and night. For three weeks we watched. Every time Sarah would topple, look like she couldn't tell the sand from the sky, Gracie would give her a nudge to show her the right way. She stayed by her side for three weeks showing her which way to go until she became well and was strong enough to swim on her own again.

Dinghy and LB

They have been together now for a long time. Dolphins are not supposed to be monogamous, but LB and Dinghy seem to need each other and prefer life that way. They have had many calves together: Cosmo Binks, KimBit, Kai, Julie, and now another little female not yet named. LB and Fonzie were often in competition. They needed to be kept separate. They were both big boys. LB was getting older. The trainers noticed he was slowing down too. He was no longer interested in playing with people from the general public. His trainer suggested we see if he might enjoy a therapy session with one of the children in the program. I had the perfect little girl in mind! She loved the dolphins, was very comfortable with them in the water and had so much fun with them.

When we came over the bridge and got into the water, it was clear that not only was Little Lou happy to see the dolphins but LB seemed happy too. He became perky and energetic. Throughout the week he would perk up every time Lou and I would get into the water. He was so happy to have her hold onto his dorsal fin as he towed her to the dock. She would giggle and squeal with delight. She was able to speak only a few words, and never in complete sentences, but one day we were in the water, waiting for LB to come and play, when without prompting Little Lou squealed and chimed, "LB, LB, Come to me!"

When he arrived to tow her through the water, play and jump through hoops, everyone was so happy! The therapy was not only good for Little Lou but for LB as well. It had lifted his spirits too! For some of those observing, it was like visiting a senior citizen. For those closest to LB, it was like visiting a beloved grandparent near the end of their life and bringing them a joyous afternoon.

LB passed of old age, not long after that. It remains a bittersweet moment for all of us, remembering that afternoon with Little Lou.

Acknowledgements

This is a memoir about love and determination. It is also about living through times of hardship and finding one's way. It is solely based on my recollection of events as best as I can summon them. If you asked everyone involved in my story to write their own version of events, you would end up with as many different stories as there are people who lived it. Therefore, I apologize for any instances where my recall falls short of perfection, but I maintain that examples of gross mistakes in this account are few — maybe even nonexistent — and of limited significance to the larger story, whose gist and message of hope are in no way diminished by minor factual error.

With regard to Fonzie's first encounter with humans, I was not present and can only imagine how he felt or what he was thinking, for, at the risk of ascribing human attributes to a marine mammal, my experience with dolphins has shown that they do indeed think and express strong emotions. Obviously, those sections of the story have been fictionalized, but they represent my interpretation of events, based on what I know of Fonzie.

I offer my thanks to Tom Madison for his careful reading, editing and tireless attention to this book and for his encouragement, which was unwavering. Many people have supported me throughout. I have been fortunate to have

[195]

friends, family and colleagues surround me with their input and feedback. I want to especially thank Mark Benjamin, Mieke Berger, Jordan Bock, Lloyd and Rick Borguss, Redmond Paul Burke MD, Robin Friday, Cynthia and Jeff Gneiser, Jim Lupino, Candace Nelms, Atsuko Otsuka, Mary Powell, Henry Root, Kate Stenson, Steph Taylor, Ted Turner and Sandy Tusick.

Special thanks as well to Maya Angelou, the Federation for the Blind, Nancy Roosevelt Ireland, and Yehuda Berg and the Kabbalah Centre for the generous privilege of allowing us the use of the quotes contained within this book. And I want to express my gratitude to Kate Ferguson and Chantal Borguss for designing the cover.

To my mother-in-law, Kiku Hanes, a source of continuous inspiration.

In memory of my loving parents, Mimi and Manny Rosen, who, if alive today, would be sitting on their pool deck proudly sharing this story with their friends and anyone else willing to listen.

Above all, I'm grateful to my husband and children for the best of times, and for standing together during the worst.

Deena Hoagland
Key Largo, Florida
18 August, 2012

[196]

About the Author

Deena and Peter Hoagland have been married since 1976. They still manage Island Dolphin Care in Key Largo, Florida — an extraordinary place that helps many children, families, and veterans from all over the world

Joe is 25 years old at the time of this writing. He lives independently, surfs and loves life and working at Island Dolphin Care.

Kate is happily married with two beautiful and healthy children.

To learn more about Island Dolphin Care,
our programs and mission, please visit our website:
www.islanddolphincare.org.

VISIT

WWW.RIFENBARY.COM

FOR MORE INFORMATION REGARDING
JAY RIFENBARY AND HIS CORE VALUE
DEVELOPMENT TRAINING.